T0358513

To our sons, the next generation
Chota and Munjimali

The Making of Modern Africa

Series Editors: Abebe Zegeye and John Higginson

Contemporary Issues in Socio-economic Reform in Zambia

Edited by
HERRICK C MPUKU
IVAN ZYUULU
Institute of Consultancy, Applied Research and Extension Studies
Copperbelt University
Kitwe, Zambia

Routledge
Taylor & Francis Group

LONDON AND NEW YORK

First published 1997 by Ashgate Publishing

Reissued 2018 by Routledge
2 Park Square, Milton Park, Abingdon, Oxon OX14 4RN
711 Third Avenue, New York, NY 10017, USA

Routledge is an imprint of the Taylor & Francis Group, an informa business

Copyright © Herrick C Mpuku and Ivan Zyuulu 1997

All rights reserved. No part of this book may be reprinted or reproduced or utilised in any form or by any electronic, mechanical, or other means, now known or hereafter invented, including photocopying and recording, or in any information storage or retrieval system, without permission in writing from the publishers.

Notice:
Product or corporate names may be trademarks or registered trademarks, and are used only for identification and explanation without intent to infringe.

Publisher's Note
The publisher has gone to great lengths to ensure the quality of this reprint but points out that some imperfections in the original copies may be apparent.

Disclaimer
The publisher has made every effort to trace copyright holders and welcomes correspondence from those they have been unable to contact.

A Library of Congress record exists under LC control number: 97072078

ISBN 13: 978-1-138-61124-5 (hbk)
ISBN 13: 978-0-429-46078-4 (ebk)

Contents

List of contributors

Amos Kambenja holds a post Secondary School Diploma in Town and Country Planning from the Zambia Institute of Technology, obtained in 1983, a B.Sc. Degree in Land Economy from the Copperbelt University, obtained in 1988 and a Master of Land Economy from the University of Aberdeen, obtained in 1992.

He has vast experience both in public and private sectors in the areas of physical planning and real estate valuation. He has undertaken field studies in the areas of land resettlement and tenure in Kenya, Ghana and Zimbabwe, sponsored by the Commonwealth Foundation, and has presented seminar papers at various fora in these areas.

Presently, Amos is a lecturer in the School Built Environment at the Copperbelt University.

C Pule Katele obtained a B A degree with Honours at Manchester University in 1969 and became a Chartered Planner in 1972.

After working for Local Government Agencies, he was assigned on several tours of duty by the Commonwealth Secretariat as a Planner and adviser in the Caribbean Basin and Southern Africa between 1979 and 1986.

He has been lecturing in the School of Built Environment of the Copperbelt University since 1992.

Dr Moses Kaunda was a graduate of the University of Zambia School Law, and acquired his Masters degree and D.Phil from the University of Cambridge, specialising in Land Law. He has written several papers on land law and reform, and taught at the Copperbelt University in the School of Built Environment. Sadly, he passed away in 1996; the editors pay tribute to a committed academic and sound intellectual.

Sylvester Mashamba is a lecturer in housing and construction at the Copperbelt University School of Built Environment. He is currently on leave at the University of Newcastle-upon-Tyne in England. He holds a Bachelor's degree in architecture from Zambia and M.Phil from England. He specialises in Third World Housing and has worked as a consultant on the formulation of Zambia's new housing policy. He has also held various senior administrative positions at the Copperbelt University.

Dr Herrick C Mpuku is a lecturer in management and economics in the School of Business and Director of the Institute of Consultancy, Applied Research and Extension Studies at the Copperbelt University. He holds a Ph.D in economics from the University of Birmingham (1992) and MBA and MSc from the Universities of Bradford and Oxford in England, and aBBA fro the University of Zambia. He is also a Fellow of the Institute of Commercial Management of the United Kingdom.

He has published and presented a number of papers on exporting and international trade, management, finance and economic theory, and served as a consultant on projects in economics, small business management and health. In 1996-1997, he was a Visiting Commonwealth Fellow at the Development and Project Planning Centre at the University of Bradford in England.

Gerry Nkombo Muuka holds a Ph.D from Edinburgh University in Scotland and MBA and BBA from the Murray State University in the US and the University of Zambia respectively. He worked as lecturer in business studies at the Copperbelt University, and he is currently teaching at Murray State University in business strategy, organisational behaviour and international management at the Grduate School of Business.

He has published papers in management and development issues in Africa; he has a special interest in the multifaceted impact of structural adjustment programmes in sub-Saharan Africa.

Dr George K Simwinga holds a PhD in management from the University of Pittsburg (1977), an MA in Public Policy and Administration from the University of Wisconsin (1972), and a BA in Economics and Public Administration from the University of Zambia (1969).

He has vast experience in management having been Director of Operations for the National Media Corporation (1990-1993); General Manager for Printpak (Z) Ltd., Times Newspapers (Z) Ltd. and Newspaper Distributors Limited (1984-1986); Superintendent, Service Training, Zambia Consolidated Copper Mines Limited (1984-1986); and Director of Training, African Centre for Monetary Studies, Association of African Central Banks, Dakar, Senegal (1978 - 1994). He has also been Dean, School of

Humanities and Social Sciences, University of Zambia (1978); Head, Department of Political and Administrative Studies, University of Zambia (1977 - 1978), and Senior Lecturer at the University of Zambia.

He has published widely, and some of his papers include: "Management and Control of State Enterprises in Zambia" in *Administration in Zambia*, edited by William Tordoff, Manchester University Press, 1980; and "The State and Public Sector Enterprises in Africa: The Need for New Orientations" in *"The African Perspectives on New International Economic Order"* United Nations University, Japan 1981.

He is currently Vice Chancellor of the Copperbelt University.

Ivan Zyuulu earned his Bachelor of Arts degree in Economics and Business Administration (April 1988) from the University of Zambia and his Master of Arts degree in Banking and Finance (November 1990) from the University of Wales, United Kingdom.

He briefly worked for the Ministry of Agriculture and Water Development, Planning Division soon after graduating from 1987 to 1988 after which he joined the Copperbelt University in 1989. He has been teaching Economics and Money and Banking to undergraduates in the School of Business and Management of Financial Institutions to Master of Business Administration (MBA) students in the same school. In addition to teaching he is currently the Head of the Business Research Group in the Institute of Consultancy, Applied Research and Extension Studies and acted as Director of the Institute in 1996-1997.

He has presented several papers at workshops and seminars. He has published two articles in the ZICA Review, a journal of the Zambia Institute of Chartered Accountants, *"The Theory and Practice of Income Smoothing,"* December, 1992 and *"Financial Innovation: Is it Constraint Induced?"* December 1993.

Acknowledgements

We are deeply indebted to the colleagues who contributed their articles for publication in this book. These are: Gerry N Muuka, Amos Kambenja, Sylvester Mashamba, Pule Katele, George K Simwinga, and posthumously, Dr Moses Kaunda (MHSRIP). The papers are based on presentations made by the authors to the School of Business seminar programme at the Copperbelt University in 1994.

Without their co-operation and commitment this work would not have been possible. Our sincere thanks also go to the Secretaries Wezi Kaira and Cynthia Mbewe for typing the papers. Others who deserve mention here are all the members of staff in the Institute of Consultancy, Applied Research and Extension Studies (ICARES), School of Business and the University Community at large. We also wish to express our gratitude to Wendy Taylor of the Development and Project Planning Centre at the University of Bradford for proof-reading the text of the book.

The list of those who have contributed to this work is obviously quite long; however, this would not be complete if we did not acknowledge our families for their support and providing a sense of belonging and responsibility during the process of preparing and editing this piece of work.

Any errors of omission or commission in the text remain the responsibilty of the authors and editors, but we all share in the successes of the work.

1 Introduction

On 31st October 1991, the people of Zambia voted overwhelmingly to change their government from the pro-socialist United National Independence Party (UNIP) to the liberal, if amorphous alliance of the newly established Movement for Multiparty Democracy (MMD).

This change of government is subject to many interpretations, but many would consider this as a verdict delivered by the people rejecting the economic and social malaise that increasingly characterised Zambia and associated with the ruling UNIP, especially during the 1980s. It may also be argued that it represents a rejection of the political and economic centralisation which were the hallmarks of UNIP policy and the excessive politicisation of all aspects of policy, institutions and society that went with it. A review of Zambia's political economic and social history over the 1970s and 1980s brings out a number of important experiences which have conditioned and influenced the peoples attitudes and actions.

Shortly after independence the government, riding on a wave of populism and nationalism introduced sweeping economic reforms that witnessed widespread nationalisation of local and international private companies in various sectors including mining, manufacturing transport and trading. The declared motive for such change was the perceived need to transfer economic power to the Zambians from foreign and sectional interests, and to promote rapid economic development through heightened state involvement and investment in the various sectors.

The law related to land was also altered to eliminate freehold tenure in favour of leasehold, and all land was vested in the president to ensure considerable state control over the dispensation and administration of land.

Social reforms were also introduced in which free education and health for all were implemented, through a rapidly expanding network of government schools and higher institutions of learning, hospitals and health centres. A social welfare system rapidly developed to support all the members of the society as private and exclusive health, educational and other social facilities were discouraged.

The country thus witnessed in the 1960s and 1970s a rapid expansion of government and parastatal institutions at a comparatively faster pace than the private sector, in investment, infrastructure and employment. With the considerable reserves available at independence and the boom in the metal markets, the government had sufficient resources to sustain these developments.

In 1972, the ruling party determined to consolidate its hold on power, instituted political reform and legislation which outlawed all other political parties, so that all those wishing to aspire to government had to so through the sole and only recognised and legal party, UNIP.

This was ostensibly intended to overcome political and social divisions in various forms which were considered a threat to national unity, survival and development. Other analysts perceived this action simply to be a manoeuvre to retain political power and control by the ruling elite.

With the change in Zambia's economic fortunes in the 1970s and little respite in the succeeding years, Zambia experienced a rapid economic decline with growing balance of payments deficits, rising inflation and unemployment, and shortages of a wide of range of consumer and intermediate goods became endemic.

As government revenue dwindled, it became increasingly difficult for government to support and subsidise the parastatal sector and government institutions such as hospitals, schools and other public services institutions.

The health and education sector practically collapsed as drugs, equipment, educational and other basic facilities rapidly declined in supply; free health and education was nothing but a hollow slogan, since the basic features of these social services were clearly absent.

As parastatals also declined in performances and lost direction through excessive politicisation, they became instruments of political patronage and agents for rewarding political loyalists. Persistent loss making supported by government largesse based on imprudent financial management became the order of the day. Such an environment of centralised political and economic power against a background of limited resources, provided a fertile ground for corruption, favouritism and other irregular practices inconsistent with high standards of morality and professionalism.

The demise of the UNIP government at the hands of a hastily constructed alliance of businessmen, intellectuals, religious leaders, students and many others dealt a telling blow to the hitherto unchallenged and socialistic leadership of UNIP, and allowed for an opportunity to experiment not only with a new government, but also with a new form of government.

The new government embraced a liberal political and economic philosophy which aimed at relegating the role of government in matters of business to a subsidiary one, and essentially that of providing the legal and regulatory framework to enable such activity take place un-hindered. Changes in various aspects of legislation and policy were therefore intended to enhance the role of individual and private enterprise as the engine of development.

The political developments of entrenching multiparty democracy through constitutional changes and supporting policies and institutions was also meant to support and foster the development of a liberal social and economic system.

This book, therefore, aims at exploring the changes that have been largely mooted since the advent of the third republic but which have also been part of a broader political, social and economic trend in thinking, advocacy and action in the country and at the global level.

This book, prepared by academicians in various areas of specialisation, has identified several key policy areas which have been the subject of reform such as land, housing, financial and economic policy, health and education, etc.

Most of the papers explore the background of the policy issues, and provide critical evaluations of new policy directions. This is with a view to providing insights and recommendations in which the efficiency and effectiveness of the socio-economic system can be enhanced to strengthen the delivery of requisite services and speed up the overall development process in the country. In a word, how best can reform benefit the people in the short, medium and the long term.

The paper by Dr Gerry Nkombo Muuka addresses itself to the basic problems of structural adjustment prescribed to developing countries by the international financial and donor community. In particular, he looks at the issue of conditionality in structural adjustment and how this element affects these programmes in developing countries. This paper deals with the

3

fundamental economic problem where, given the paucity of resources, countries are expected to effect a drastic reorganisation of their economies while depending heavily on financial support of otherwise well-meaning but stringent sympathisers from outside.

The paper therefore provides a general setting for most of the discussion that follows. Chapter 3 by Ivan Zyuulu considers the innovations and reforms that are likely to take place in the Zambian financial system. It is apparent that the efficiency with which the financial system functions in mobilising and allocating resources to investment opportunities is an important factor in the development process. In his paper, Mr Zyuulu demonstrates how, under liberalisation, deregulation and changes in technology, financial institutions can provide new instruments and services to survive and grow.

Amos Kambenja looks at the problem of land and its relationship to economic development in Zambia. He presents the conceptual background of the interrelationships and outlines the two ideologically different models of land tenure of Kenya and Tanzania.

He argues that changes in the system of land tenure by themselves cannot guarantee economic success; rather broad-based policy improvements encompassing the strengthening of land administration and providing supporting services and infrastructure are more crucial than mere changes in tenancy.

In a sequel to Amos Kambenja' s paper, Dr Moses Kaunda evaluates the process of formulating land policy in Zambia. He surveys the background of land administration and policy from pre-independence Zambia. He presents the major considerations in the development of land policy given the structure of the Zambian land law presently. He argues that policy should cover issues of ownership, allocation, use and transfer of land for it to have a clear meaning and use to the society.

Dr Kaunda clearly indicates his preference for the lease hold system over the freehold on the grounds that the 99 year lease is sufficiently long to allow investors to recoup their investments, and may, therefore, not deter investment and the development that may arise.

Sylvester Mashamba's piece examines the successes and pitfalls of housing policy in pre and post-independence Zambia. He considers how the vicissitudes in policy have contributed to expansion of housing units of various categories over a period of time, and how and why stagnation and squalor in housing have also emerged in Zambia.

4

He argues that the new shelter policy being evolved by the government should ensure a judicious mix of market forces and government intervention to support the development of desirable and acceptable housing units to the majority of Zambians.

Mr Mashamba's paper is followed by a paper by C Pule Katele. He introduces the concepts of sustainable development and their relevancy to the development and growth of human settlements in Zambia. Considering past and present failures in the attainment of acceptable urbanisation patterns in Zambia, the author provides goals, objectives and strategies for sustaining development of human settlements during the 21st century.

In the paper on health reforms in chapter eight, Dr Herrick C Mpuku reviews the background to the country's health reforms and analyses recent developments d policy directions and their implications in the provision of health services. By identifying constraints and bottlenecks in the reform programme, he is able to recommend administrative and financial mechanisms as well as management actions which could ensure a smooth institutional reform while assuring a financially sustainable and socially acceptable health care system.

Dr George K Simwinga in chapter nine draws from the experiences of the Copperbelt University to exemplify the stresses and strains that are experienced in higher education during the process of reforms, especially given changing socio-economic circumstances in the 1990s. He feels that the best way to address the human dimension in the development of the University is to democratise the institution by enhancing representation, promoting electivity and improving communication vertically and horizontally in the University system.

He argues that in trying to meet the raised expectation in the University Community, there is a danger that the core mission of the University may be lost. He therefore, calls for continued financial support for higher education, and the Universities in particular, as they strive to democratise and meet the expectations of their members, to accomplish the broader goal of effective teaching and provision of public services.

In conclusion, we should point out that the unifying theme of the papers in this issue is that national and gobal change has necessitated the socio-economic transformation of our country, which phoenomenon we must examine in all its facets.

With a modern political system of open debate, better and more efficient communication than has been the case before and a more erudite and informed public, the challenge of change and the opportunities of transformation to meet the social and economic aspirations of a new generation at the dawn of the new millennium, are immense.

2 Accounting for less than optimal performance of structural adjustment programmes in sub-saharan African countries

Gerry Nkombo Muuka

Introduction

There is considerable debate, in the literature, regarding the performance of economies supported by the World Bank (Bank) and International Monetary Fund (IMF) backed structural adjustment programmes (SAPs). There is controversy surrounding--- but not restricted to--- criteria for assessing the impact of SAPs; whether the mere implementation of wide facets of conditionality--- as is the case with Zambia after 1992--- is in itself a measure of success; and secondly there is the obvious difficulty of disentangling the effects of SAP measures from other factors which have an equally important impact on economic performance, such as the effect of drought in Zambia in recent years.

Rather than enter the wider debate alluded to above, this paper focuses attention on some of the causes for the less-than impressive results of structural adjustment programmes in Sub-Saharan Africa (SSA). This presupposes there is agreement about what SAPs are meant to achieve in the first place. The paper starts with an outline of this, discussing the general goals of SAPs.

General goals of structural adjustment programmes

Most countries undertake Bank-Fund reforms because of stagnating declining, or negative growth in their economies. In more specific terms, countries undertaking structural adjustment programmes are those that, against a background of the poor state of their economies, need to do a number of things, viz;

(a) Need to encourage non-traditional Exports, (NTEs). In Zambia's case, NTEs are loosely defined as all non-copper exports; copper still accounts for over 85 percent of export earnings. Zambia's non-copper exports comprise both primary and manufactured (visible) products, as well as invisibles in services such as tourism and energy. Under structural adjustment, diversification of Zambia's export base would normally fall under the Bank's "policy-based" lending--- which aims to strengthen recipients' external payments positions and to accelerate development.

(b) Aim to reduce or eliminate balance of payments (BOP) deficits. The aim here is to get the economy to produce and sell more than it imports--- a positive trade balance--- as a necessary pre-condition toward reducing the overall balance of payments deficit.

(c) Need to achieve structural changes that will limit or prevent future payments and stabilisation problems--- thereby making the economy less vulnerable to future shocks. Under Zambia's SAP, for instance, broadening the production and export bases beyond copper is aimed inter alia at lessening the impact of an unexpected copper price shock--- that is a sudden drop in the price of copper, which is externally determined.

(d) Switch production from non-tradables to tradables. Woodward (1992: p289) defines non-tradables as goods which cannot be exported or imported internationally from or to a particular market for economic, practical, or administrative reasons, such as national or international trade regulations, inadequate transport infrastructure, or perishable nature of the product. A major goal of adjustment is to try to encourage producers to produce more tradable and less non-tradable goods, and consumers to consume less tradable and more non-tradable goods so as to strengthen the Balance of Payments. This switch is considered desirable in most Sub-Sahara African (SSA) countries because of the anti-agricultural and anti-rural sector bias of previous government policies, believed to be responsible for wide-spread under-utilisation of agricultural productive capacity. And as we shall see later, the most pervasive instrument for achieving the required switch in the structure of price and other such incentives is devaluation of local currencies.

e) Need to reduce levels of foreign debt, inflation and unemployment.

At the micro or sector level, SAPs aim to increase capacity utilisation rates, increase outward orientation while reducing imports and import dependence, as well as to diversify the destination of NTEs. Finally, increasing both inter-sectoral and intra-sectoral linkages is a major goal.

The overall aim of the above SAP targets is to induce, in the economy concerned, a higher and sustainable rate of economic growth. On the eve of undertaking serious adjustment in 1983, Zambia for instance was experiencing a macro-economic crisis that needed to be addressed.

A quick look at the above reveals some ambiguity, on the part of both the Bank and Fund, between what constitutes a goal/objective and strategy. Broadening the NTE-base, for example, is indicated as an objective, when in fact it is a strategy towards achieving the goal of economic growth and development. In Zambia's case, it would mean that simply increasing the nature and number of non-traditional exporters constitutes success---because the "objective" of broadening the export base will have been achieved (Muuka 1993: p83). The number of exporters and/or exportable products may grow, but that does not necessarily lead to a corresponding increase in total export receipts. Clarity between what constitutes an objective or goal and a strategy is therefore self-evidently essential.

Having outlined some of the goals of SAPs, the next logical question centres around how the Bank, Fund and programme countries evaluate the performance of SAPs. This is discussed next.

Criteria for assessing the impact of SAPs

There are three major criteria for assessing the performance of SAPs. All three, unfortunately, have short-comings.

Before-after approach

There are those who think the country's economic performance before the introduction of adjustment should be compared with its performance after the introduction of the programme. Such a methodology would be easy to apply, involving assessment of whether the programme was associated with an improvement over the initial situation. The problem with this school of thought, observes Killick (1992a: p3), is that there are numerous and varying time lags between policy changes and their effects and that world economic conditions that impinge upon an economy's performance are not static.

Actual-versus-targets approach

The argument here is that the results of the programme should be compared to the targets set in the policy frame-work paper (PFP) and national budgets at the start of the programme. Killick (ibid.) again contends that this can do no more than give us some pointers, for the additional reasons that the targets themselves may have been unrealistic, or arbitrary. Also, such quantified targets may be no better than the models which generate them in simulations, so that discrepancies between targets and actualities may be a result of poorly performing models rather than intrinsically unsatisfactory economic results (Killick, Malik and Manuel 1991: p6).

With-versus-without-programme approach

This is also known as the control-group approach. Should the performance of economies with adjustment programmes be compared with a control group of non-programme countries? Alternatively, should programme results be compared with the counter-factual --- what would have happened in the absence of the programme? Commander (1989) argues that simply contrasting the performance of economies with SAPs against those without such programmes indicates a diffuse and ambiguous set of outcomes, with Killick pointing out that the central difficulty is to select a control group that is truly comparable. Killick (1992a: p4) argues:

> The essential problem in programme assessment is that of the counter-factual, how can we judge what would have happened in the absence of the programme? There are other difficulties too: how to disentangle the effects of the programme from the effects of the credits provided in support of IFI programmes, and how to handle different degrees of programme implementation across countries? There is also the quandary of deciding the period over which a programme should be

assessed: do we look simply at results during the programme, or over some longer period?

A final problem with the counter-factual is its subjectivity. A lot of assumptions and judgements would be necessary, introducing yet more impossible-to-prove-and-resolve dilemmas.

Some of the causes for the unsatisfactory performance of SAPs are rooted in the nature of conditionality. It is therefore necessary, before discussing these causes, to say something about the layers and instruments of conditionality, implementation and dealing with pricing of products and services to be sold by the project and its management. This was then extended to other sectors. Now, with the introduction of structural adjustment lending (in 1979), it extends to the entire economy of a country. The centre of attention is the investment programme, system of incentives, pricing, financial liberalisation, and trade liberalisation. The types of conditionalities which come with such programmes include:

Growth conditionality: in application during the last six years or so, this focuses on giving a free hand and incentives to the private sector of the economy, including privatisation of state-owned enterprises (SOEs) as much as possible, rationalisation of the rest, and again trade liberalisation.

Cross conditionality: here, lending decisions of each agency depend on the borrower having met the loan conditions of some other agency. This is now in increasing use, and it involves private as well as official lenders. The breakdown in arrangements between a borrowing country and any one of these agencies--- in particular the Bank and Fund--- can have a "domino effect" in relation with all other agencies.

An example of cross conditionality is when, early in 1987, the British government agreed to extend a loan to Zambia conditional upon an agreement being reached with the Fund. Immediately it became known that no agreement had been reached, the British announced that the money was no longer available (Fundanga, 1989).

The increasing, and changing, nature of conditionality has been coined as the Christmas tree approach to conditionality. Killick (1987: p27) points out that there has been a convergence of roles between the Bank and Fund, whose effect has been a conditionality explosion. He argues:

There is presently more policy conditionality around, it is more intense and it is of a wider range. The cause for this is the move of the Bank into policy-based lending through structural adjustment loans (SALs), and sectoral loans which carry similar conditions. In addition the Fund has increasingly added supply-side to the conventional demand-side conditionality. There has also been a movement in both institutions towards per-conditions, for example in terms of exchange rate adjustments.

Major elements or instruments of conditionality

Among the major elements of conditionality are exchange rate policy; public sector restructuring and privatisation; liberalisation and commercialisation; as well as political conditionality. The latter three are discussed below.

Public sector restructuring and privatisation

Public sector is the generic term used to describe not only the traditional government ministries and agencies, but more so government's participation in, and involvement with, parastatals/state-owned enterprises.

In responding to Africa's plea for development assistance to counter the overall economic crisis over the last two decades, the Bank and the Fund have pointed out the following short-comings as directly attributable to the nature of the public sector on the continent (World Bank, 1984). First, that public sector responsibilities and employment have become unmanageably large. Effectiveness and efficiency have thus been gravely compromised especially in marketing, transport, education and health, and manufacturing. Second, that the failure by governments to shed-off the "political role" of parastatals has meant an effective breeding ground for inertia, and corruption. Parastatals have been pressured, in many countries, to increase employment, to deliver outputs at low prices to key groups, and to shape investment decisions other than with economic and financial returns in view; most of them, inevitably, have become financial burdens.

Third, managerial and technical capacities have not been sufficiently established tending for the most part to be mirrored along government lines. Instead of encouraging it, parastatals have stifled individual initiative. Fourth, to the extent that African governments have a history of uniform, and sometimes massive wage increases for both the civil service and the state-owned sector, this has contributed to rising inflation.

Actual conditionality in this area calls for dramatic reductions in government involvement in the economy---through, among others, deregulation and privatisation. One of the many arguments for privatisation is that somehow it will restrain the government from "political meddling" in the enterprise once ownership changes hands (Rodrik 1990: p943). Yet another major argument is that under the right economic environment, private ownership should improve both allocative and technical efficiency. This is so because, going by the property-rights argument, people who have a majority stake in the business have incentives to run it efficiently, and will want to maximise profits and minimise wastages.

Pruning of the civil service and a general wage freeze to help control inflation have also been high on the traditional Bank-Fund conditionality menu.

Liberalisation and commercialisation

Reusse (1987: p299) defines liberalisation as:

> The process of removing legal prohibitions to private trade in selected commodities and taking other actions aimed at facilitating the functioning of the private sector, with the objective of placing greater reliance on the market to allocate resources. In all countries, the state is always involved in setting the basic rules under which markets operate and in determining what may or may not be legitimately traded. In this sense, liberalisation is a process of redefining property rights---i.e. including the relative roles of the public and private sectors in the economy--not a process of simply getting the state out of the market. In this sense it is a somewhat broader concept than privatisation.

Even though structural adjustment is a multifaceted process, liberalisation--- or "market-oriented reforms"--- has increasingly taken centre stage in Bank-Fund conditionality. Its major case rests on the arguments that: (i) allocative efficiency can be improved by lifting controls in markets for commodities, credit, and foreign exchange (Rodrik 1990: p937); (ii) it reduces monopoly power; (iii) it increased the incentive to innovate and (iv) that it leads to greater responsiveness to consumer needs.

13

Manifestations of liberalisation   In summary, liberalisation entails the following:

- The adjustment/devaluation and/or floating of hitherto fixed exchanges rates. The maintenance of a realistic exchange rate, along with other incentives and facilities for non-traditional exports, is supposed to produce a highly open but strong economy. In the context of export liberalisation Donges and Hiemenz (1991: p215) argue for instance that the way to adopt an outward orientation is to expose the domestic economy to international competition for the purpose of improving allocative efficiency, capturing economies of scale, managing risk through export diversification, and accelerating technological innovation. They argue that two conditions are useful for the success of an out-ward oriented strategy: the substitution of price signals for administrative controls and the adjustment of domestic relative prices so that they conform to relative prices internationally.

- The decontrol of internal price system as well as external and internal trade flows.

- Removal of legal restrictions on private entrepreneurship.

- Abolition of state enterprises and monopolies in both production and marketing.

- Reforming banking policy is aimed at redirecting the flow of savings from the public to the private sector (Mamdani 1990: p430), including interest rate decontrol.

- Cutting the state budget, including the removal of all consumer subsidies and other social expenditures.

- Removal of import restrictions: this aspect of trade liberalisation is premised on over-protection of domestic industries being responsible for breeding inefficiency. The exposure of indigenous firms to competition is supposed to force them to improve their efficiency.

- Diversification into non-traditional exports to reduce instability in export earnings, and strengthening the incentive system for production and exports and removing distortions and rigidities.

- Reduction in money supply accompanied by a general public sector wage and salary freeze to control inflation.

- Divestment of hitherto state or parastatal marketing operations.

The foregoing conditionalities may not be exhaustive, though the list does shed more light on the thinking of the Bank and Fund whenever the concept of liberalisation is mentioned during "consultative" meetings with would-be aid/loan recipients.

Political conditionality

Increasingly conspicuous on the conditionality menu in the 1990s, is political conditionality, defined by Moore (1993: p.1) as the tying of official aid disbursements to the quality of government (or governance) that aid recipients provide. In the view of the World Bank (1989: p.60), history suggests that political legitimacy and consensus are a pre-condition for sustainable development. Underlying the litany of Africa's development problems, the Bank argues, is a crisis of governance. By governance is meant the exercise of political power to manage a nation's affairs. Because countervailing power has been lacking--- the Bank argues--- state officials in many countries have served their own interests without fear of being called to account. This environment, concludes the Bank, cannot readily support a dynamic economy. Hence the current insistence by the donor community on democratic reforms as a pre-condition for further assistance to third world nations.

Why the current "rush" towards political conditionality? The Institute of Development Studies (IDS) devotes an entire volume--- number 24 of January 1993--- to a discussion of political conditionality and "good government". Edited by Mick Moore, the various contributors seem to agree that the current, unprecedented, wave of political conditionality has one major source: the collapse of the Soviet Block and of Communist rule throughout Eastern Europe and the former Soviet Union, which has put an end to the competition between East and West for influence in the third world (Moore 1993: p1).

The uses of aid need no longer be shaped by geo-political considerations and compromises. Stereo-typically, Moore argues, that it is no longer necessary or possible to support what he calls nasty authoritarian regimes on the grounds that they are the only feasible alternative to local Communists and/or Soviet, Cuban or Chinese influence.

Having thus provided the necessary background, the rest of this paper is devoted to advancing a few causes for the less than optimal results of SAPs.

Accounting for less-than optimal SAP results in SSA countries

Structural adjustment programmes may fail to achieve the desired results because of a hostile global environment; more or less technical considerations relating to the design of economic policy packages; and matters relating to relationships between aid agencies and recipient governments. We elaborate the last two first, before looking at other causes.

Technical considerations

As Killick (1992: p7) points out, the design of policy packages to foster economic growth is no simple matter. There are many trade-offs in making policy in this area, posing difficult choices. There are also many complexities: economic policies should be viewed as a system, and complicated interactions occur between policy and target variables (including time-lags between policy decisions and their effects), with the indirect effects of measures often quite different from their direct impacts. The construction of adjustment programmes, in other words, is a difficult, complex business. Another area of difficulty relates to the reconciliation of the demand-management approach of IMF stabilisation programmes and the supply-oriented thrust of Bank structural adjustment programmes. Killick (ibid.) argues:

> There's a danger that IMF- type programmes which envisage large reductions in imports will erode export supply responses, to say nothing of the costs imposed by way of output foregone... To put the case in more general terms, tensions can arise between demand-management

and supply-oriented programmes as a result of differences in the requirements for programme success in respect of (a) import levels, (b) volumes and terms of domestic credit and, (c) government expenditures on economic services and/or capital formation... an implication of this is that the two International Finance Institutions (IFIs) may sometimes give differing advice to governments.

Abbey (1991: p523), agrees that those caught in the middle of Bank and Fund advice are not amused by such disagreements, particularly when there are legitimate policy conflicts to be resolved.

Donor-recipient relations

Killick (ibid.) believes the danger here is that the very fact of conditionality, and the nature of the donor-recipient relationship which it implies, will undermine programme effectiveness:

> Much hinges on the extent to which there's genuine agreement between the IFIs and the government in question about the desirability of the programme and its provisions... One source of difficulty here may be a mis-match of values and objectives... The IFIs have to satisfy their major shareholders, who often take a lively interest in what loans are made to whom and for what, and who sometimes seek to use their influence on the IFI Boards to promote their own foreign policy and/or commercial interests. The IFIs see their loans to any one country in the context of a far larger set of lending activities, so that decisions about policy changes in one country are influenced by what is being done elsewhere. Governments and Ministers, on the other hand, are supposed to concentrate on promoting the national interest. Additionally or alternatively, they may have other worries: how to win (or avoid!) an election, how to keep the army happy, and how to reward supporters and deal with the opposition.

In short, government and IFI objectives may not match up and this may lead to disagreement about policies. Killick and Malik (1991: P35) point out that where adversarial relationships between governments and the Bank-Fund exist, they are likely to contribute to non-implementation of policy conditions, resulting in ineffectual programmes.

Exogenous determinants

Killick and Malik (ibid: p33) further argue that there is evidence that both the gravity of the initial situation and the intrusion of external and other unforeseen shocks are major reasons for programme failure. This, they believe, is partly because of the great vulnerability of many of the economies in question. Programme break-down is associated with particularly adverse terms of trade experiences.

The "ownership of SAPs" question

Berg 1991: p217) suggests that political and bureaucratic consensus is even more uncommon:

> Agreements negotiated and signed by ministers of finance or planning are implemented by sectoral ministries. Sometimes these ministries are only perfunctorily consulted; often they are in deep disagreement with the spirit and particulars of the reform programme.

He indicates another difficulty: that conditionality gives the impression that programmes are being imposed upon a reluctant government even when they may not be. Such a public perception may undermine the legitimacy of the programme and, therefore, the likelihood that it will be successfully implemented and sustained. Even where that does not occur, extensive IFI determination of the content of a programme will weaken what the Bank calls the government's sense of "ownership" of the programme, which may well be the most important determinant of its success. Such circumstances, concludes Killick (ibid), are liable to throw up programmes which governments do not regard as their own and which, therefore, they will implement only at the inescapable minimum.

Infrastructural inadequacies

As expected, the Bank and Fund do offer explanations for the less than optimal SAP results. The World Bank (1988: p3) argues that the supply response to adjustment in SSA has been slow because of the legacy of deep-seated structural problems. The Bank admits that inadequate infrastructure, poorly developed markets, rudimentary industrial sectors, and severe institutional and managerial weaknesses in the public and private sectors have proved unexpectedly serious as constraints to better performance in SSA.

Policy sustainability and financing adequacy

The Bank (ibid.) further admits that the speed of the supply response determines sustainability:

> A strong export response helped the continuation of reforms in Turkey. By contrast, policy reversals in Zambia resulted partly from the lags in export growth. The supply response also depends on greater institutionalisation of reforms, thereby strengthening their credibility to investors. Also, complementary reforms to reduce internal regulations and factor market rigidities are sometimes essential for a stronger supply response.

On the question of financing, the Bank's view is that financing and sustainability of adjustment programmes are mutually reinforcing, citing inadequate funding as part of the reason for the policy reversal in Zambia in 1987 while Ghana's effort has been helped by the availability of finance.

Severe behavioural and attitudinal changes implicit in SAPs

In addition to the more technical issues of SAPs argued in the literature, there are also the behavioural and attitudinal changes needed for SAP success but which, in reality, take a long time to come about. The people of Africa, like everybody else, are mostly conservative and slow to adjust. It is easy to fly into a country and tell people to devalue their currency and then fly away. But there is the problem that the people left behind are the ones who have to stay alive. They have to make all the painful adjustments. And the more marginal the economy is as most SSA economies invariably are, the more the downside risks and resistance to the kind of attitudinal and behavioural changes, SAPs take for granted but that are critical for success.

Dilemmas of conditionality

Stevens and Killick (1991: p6) offer what they consider to be four main dilemmas facing both donors and recipients when designing adjustment policies; these are further reasons why SAPs have not scored convincing successes. The four dilemmas are;

(i) The provisions derived from mainstream policy theory are sometimes an inappropriate technology, yet the donor community is constrained in making it more appropriate: the homogeneity of the Bank-Fund conditionality menu, despite the heterogeneity of recipient countries, reflects the fact that conditionality has become a key instrument for translating into developing country practice the policy recommendations of Western-based economist. This Stevens and Killick argue gives rise to a danger that conditionality may incorporate elements of "inappropriate technology", with the IFIs/donors facing intellectual political and resource constraints in adapting this into more appropriate forms.

(ii) Closely related to the above argument is the one that the design of effective economic policies is a highly complex matter and heavily dependent on the specifics of the economy in question, yet there is a strong institutional imperative for off-the-peg solutions and standard recipes.

(iii) The measures contained in conditionality agreements are undermined by their externally driven nature, and the fact that they are usually undertaken in crisis conditions further reduces the likelihood of successful implementation.

(iv) That adjustment, which is the objective of conditionality, is most needed where it is most difficult. On this issue the two authors argue that the capacity to adjust is a rising function of development--- up to a point. It is particularly weak in developing countries.

Political conditionality

Riddel (1992: p61) points out another dilemma of conditionality: that the governments through which the Fund operates rarely represent all their inhabitants. Democracy, he says, is found in only a few countries in SSA, with the norm being some form of dictatorial rule by either the military or one-party leaders. The curious paradox is whereby the Bank and Fund require a strong state in order to implement the SAP, while weakening the government through "political conditionality".

Nature of SSA's major current export markets

Under current World Bank and IMF (Bank-Fund) SAPs Zambia is only one of may programme countries being encouraged (sometimes forced) to assume an out-ward looking strategy. For most of Sub-Saharan Africa the major export products (primary agricultural and mineral products) and markets outside Africa are--- for economic and historical reasons--- identical in Zambia's.

If most of them succeed in increasing exports to Western markets--- even assuming successive relaxation of protectionist tendencies there---there is the ominous possibility that the resulting surge of both primary and manufactured exports could cause a glut on those markets. This would lead either to too low prices and losses from exports *(the so-called fallacy of composition argument)* or the re-imposition of import-barriers in these countries to protect their own local industries from cheap third world imports.

Another problem is the identity/similarity of SAP programmes in SSA. Most of these countries pursue similar adjustment programmes and face the same Bank and Fund conditionalities. As part of SAP they will aim to reduce imports. In 1991 Zambia's exports to Zimbabwe had to reduce its imports in line with its own tight foreign exchange (forex) situation. This amounted to a loss of export earnings for Zambia. This is one of the conflicts with regard to the macro-goals of Bank-Fund structural adjustment programmes, and does apply to SSA countries generally.

The time factor in structural adjustment

Time is a vital factor with regard to the way in which economies adjust. Macro-economic financial adjustments--- such as in exchange and interest rates--- can be made fairly quickly, but to actually get industries to change their products, diversify markets, investment patterns and distribution channels takes years because the changes take a long time to work through the economy. Also because of the different rates at which different parts of the economy adjust, trade tends to be affected more rapidly than production.

Under devaluation, for instance, the cost effects are felt immediately in terms of rising costs of imported inputs and intermediate products.

Gulhati (1989: p51) argues, for instance, that SAPs require a combination of "getting the prices right" and complementary technical, managerial, attitudinal, and institutional changes that are time consuming--- and warns that attempts to force the pace of change may not be the best way to proceed in SSA.

4-D syndrome undermines reforms

Countries such as Zambia that have been victims of the 4-D syndrome--- debt, disease, dependence on imported raw materials and primary exports --- have discovered that the persistence of macro-economic instability can undermine the success of reforms.

Problems in the global adjustment process

A far more serious problem at the international level deals with what Woodward (1992: p148) describes as problems in the global adjustment process, specifically what he calls "the asymmetry of macro-economic adjustment". Woodward reminds us that the process of macro-economic adjustment---which in turn affects micro level/enterprise adjustment--- centres around the pressure on countries such as Zambia with BOP deficits to reduce these deficits, without any equivalent pressure on nations with BOP surpluses to reduce their surpluses.

If Woodward's useful argument is taken--- that one country's BOP deficit is by trade definition another country's BOP surplus just as one country's imports are another country's exports--- then a second form of asymmetry in the adjustment process becomes important: the vast differences in economic and political power of different countries and groups of countries, especially between developed and developing countries. While the Funds gives policy advice to developed countries in its annual consultations with them, there is a fundamental difference between the Fund's relationship with its developed members and that with its developing members. The relationship between the Fund and developed members is effectively that between an institution and its major shareholders. Its relationship with developing countries is essentially that between a lender and its actual or potential borrowers. This inequality, Woodward argues, is further compounded by the technical and institutional capacities of the two groups: Fund discussions with developed countries are essentially a dialogue between equals; while the more limited capacity for economic analysis in most developing nations puts the Fund in a more dominant position there.

Bird and Killick (see ODI 1993: p4) take a similar view, arguing that ultimately it is the Western governments which decide the Fund's policies and which determine its stance towards developing countries. They conclude (ibid) that:

> Since the USA exerts a particularly strong influence, disproportionate to its importance in world trade, to say nothing of its record as persistent producer of the world's largest budget deficit, the policies of the Clinton administration will be crucial in this regard.

The asymmetry is further compounded by the demand-orientation of Fund programmes, requiring adjusting developing countries to reduce demand or imports as part of conditionality. This situation--- as Woodward rightly observes---tends to push developing deficit nations into reducing their demand as a means of external adjustment, but surplus nations under no equivalent pressure to allow an off-setting increase in their demand. When deficit nations represent a large proportion of the world economy---as they currently do---the net effect is to slow down the growth of demand, and thus of income, in the world economy.

The above scenario leads to a reduction in the rate of growth of demand for the exports---both primary and manufactured---of countries like Zambia that are trying to adjust.

Conclusion

An attempt has been made, in this paper, to advance some of the reasons for the still unimpressive performance of Sub-Saharan African economies undergoing World Bank and IMF-inspired structural reforms. This discussion is preceded by an examination of both the goals of structural adjustment programmes and general criteria for their assessment.

Infrastructural inadequacies --- manifest in rudimentary industrial structures and severe institutional and managerial weaknesses in SSA --- were identified as one of many contributing factors towards SSA's poor adjustment record. Although no ranking of these factors is attempted in the paper, due prominence is given to such other serious factors as the dilemmas of conditionality, the 4-D syndrome, the time factor in structural adjustment, as well as problems emanating from the global adjustment process.

Bibliography

Abbey J (1991) 'Lessons of Experience and the future of adjustment lending' in Thomas V, et al (eds) op. cit.

Avramovic A (1989), 'Conditionality, Facts, Theory and Policy--- Contribution to the Reconstruction of the International Financial System', in Onimode B (ed.) op.cit.

Berg E (1991), Comments on 'The Design and Implementation of conditionality in Adjustment Programmes', in Thomas V, et al, op. cit.

Commander S (ed.) (1989), *Structural Adjustment and Agriculture- Theory and Practice in Africa and Latin America*, ODI, London.

Donges B J and Hiemenz U (1991), 'Export Liberalisation', in Krause and Hihwan (eds), op. cit.

Export Board of Zambia (EBZ) *Exporter Audits*, 1978-1992.

Fundanga C (1991), 'The Role of the IMF and World Bank in Zambia', in Onimode B (ed.), op. cit.

Havnevik K J (ed.). (1987), *The IMF and the World Bank in Africa; Conditionality, Impact and Alternatives*, Scandinavian Institute of African Studies, Uppsala.

Helleiner G K (1992), 'Structural Adjustment and Long-Term Development in SSA', in Stewart, Lall and Wangwe (eds) op. cit.

Killick T (1987), 'Reflections on the IMF/World Bank Relationship' in Havnevik K H (ed.). op. cit.

Killick T, Malik M and Manuel M (1991), 'What can we know about the effects of IMF Programmes?' *ODI Working Paper no. 47*, London.

Killick T and Malik M (1991), Country Experiences with IMF Programmes in the 1980s, *ODI Working Paper no. 48*, London.

Killick T (1992), 'Problems and Sources of difficulty with Adjustment Conditionality', Paper presented at the National Conference on Zambia's SAP held in Kitwe, Zambia, 21-23 March.

Krause L B and Kihwan K (eds) (1991), *Liberalisation in the process of economic development*, University of California Press, Berkeley.

Mamdani M (1990), 'Uganda: Contradictions of the IMF Programme and Perspective', *Development and Change*, Vol. 21, no. 3.

Muuka G N (1993),' The Impact of Zambia's 1983-93 Structural Adjustment Programme on Business Strategy', *Ph.D. Thesis*, The University of Edinburgh.

Moore M (ed.) (1993), 'Good Government?', *IDS Bulletin*, Vol. 24.

ODI (1993), 'Does the IMF really help Developing Countries?' Briefing paper on the results of a research project undertaken by Graham Bird and Tony Killick, ODI, London.

Onimode B (ed.), (1989), *The IMF, the World Bank and the African Debt: The Economic and Social Impact*, vols. 1 & 2, Zed Books, London.

Prendergast R and Singer H W (eds) 1991), *Development Perspectives for the 1990s*, Macmillan, London.

Riddell J B (1992) 'Things Fall Apart Again: Structural Adjustment Programmes in Sub-Saharan Africa', Journal of Modern African Studies vol. 30, no. 1.

Reusse E (1987), 'Liberalisation and Agricultural Marketing: Recent causes and effects in Third World economies', *Food Policy*, November.

Rodrik D (1990), 'How should Structural Adjustment Programmes be Designed?', *World Development*, vol. 18 no. 7.

Stevens C and Killick T (1991), 'The EC and Structural Adjustment', in Prendergast and Singer (eds) op. cit.

Stewart F, Lall S and Wangwe S (eds.) (1992*)*, *Alternative Development Strategies in SSA*, Macmillan, Hampshire.

Thomas V, Chhibber A, Dailami M and Jaime de Melo (1991), *Restructuring Economies in Distress*, World Bank, Washington, D.C.

Woodward D (1992), *Debt, Adjustment and Poverty in Developing Countries*, Pinter Publishers, London, and Save and Children.

World Bank (1984), *Toward Sustained Development in Sub-Saharan Africa*: A Joint Programme of Action, Washington, D.C.

World Bank (1988), *Adjustment Lending: An Evaluation of Ten Years of Experience*, Washington, D.C.

World Bank (1989), *Sub-Saharan Africa: From Crisis to Sustainable Growth - A Long-Term Perspective Study*, Washington, D.C.

3 Financial innovation and reform in Zambia

Ivan Zyuulu

Introduction

The key term that summarises the route to survival and indeed success in the financial services industry during the past three decades is "financial innovation." During this period, the industry has seen substantial changes in technology, regulation and/or deregulation, and the industry itself has changed due to institutionalisation, globalisation and indeed securitisation. In addition, competition has been increasing as the services offered by banks and non-bank financial institutions have become more and more identical. Financial innovation is one of the major forces that has made firms in the financial services industry survive or be successful despite these rigorous changes in the industry.

The objective of this paper is to look at the question of why financial innovation arises. That is, what explanations can we give as to what brings about financial innovation or what induces it? In our attempt to answer this question we shall focus our discussion around the hypothesis that all financial innovation is constraint-induced. We shall begin by defining the concept, and thereafter discuss the various theories that are given in the literature to explain financial innovation. After this we shall relate financial innovation to the Zambian context with respect to the reforms that have been undertaken in the financial services industry in the recent past.

The concepts

Innovation is usually confused with invention, yet these two words mean completely different things though they are related. It is imperative, therefore, to distinguish them here. An invention is simply the act of finding new ways to do useful or profitable things, usually cheaper and more efficient means of doing them. An innovation on the other hand is the act of putting an invention into practice (Kane, 1981, p358). In other words, innovation can be said to be the first commercial application, or production, of a new process or product. It is usually a "surprise change" in that it is unanticipated and unforecastable. The successful practical implementation of an invention by way of introducing new products and techniques into the economic system, if successful, results in increased capability of doing something that could not be done before, or at least not so well, or so economically. The capacity of the economic system to provide wanted goods and services is increased.

The other core term for the latter part of the discussion is financial reform. It simply refers to changes in the financial system. Literally, it means to make the financial system better by removing or putting right faults or errors. Usually this would be a movement from an over-controlled system to a liberal or less-controlled one. The opposite is equally true. Movement from a very liberal system to a more regulated one is also done through financial reform. Reform therefore is merely a process of moving from one state to another for the purposes of our discussion. It constitutes a set of deliberate policies that ensures that the changes take place in the financial system.

Theories of financial innovation

A number of theories have been advanced in an effort to explain why financial innovation occurs.

The Schumpeterian theory

In the Schumpeterian view, though Schumpeter himself did not explicitly consider financial innovations as an integral part of general economic evolution, financial innovation can be thought to be a reaction to impulses coming from the real sector. As W. L. Silber (1975) noted, innovation of money responds to stimulus in the real sector and in turn influences the potential path of real economic activity. In support of the same view, Minsky (Podoloski, 1986) states that institutional innovation is one aspect of a dynamic economy, and money-market innovations occur in response to the need of a growing economy.

For Schumpeter, profit seeking entrepreneurs undertake technological innovations to secure a temporary monopolistic advantage over their rivals. These innovations, according to him, lead to "new men" organising "new firms" and thereby stimulating economic expansion. Therefore, financial development is an integral part of economic evolution. After all, in his view, expansion that is initiated by technical innovations is financed not by saving, but by credit creation, which is considered to be the monetary complement of innovation. He says that there is a logical relation between innovation and credit creation by banks. The essential element underlying the Schumpeterian process of economic evolution is the financing of enterprise associated with technological innovations, and the concomitant generation of means of payment (Podoloski, 1986, pp181-183).

Schumpeter's view can be summarised by saying that the expansions of credit and money, together with institutional changes in the banking sector, are related to expansion in the real sector, brought about by technological innovation. Financial innovation allows for flexibility in financing which enables an economy to increase its real activity without necessarily raising the level of some conventional money. What we can deduce from Schumpeter's works is that there is a fundamental connection between change in the real sector and the financial sector. Economic growth therefore results in innovations in the financial sector. This theory links financial change with technological and institutional development in the real sector.

Kane's circumventive innovation theory

This theory specifically looks at regulation as being the factor that induces financial innovation. Financial innovation is used as a device to by-pass or circumvent monetary control. It is based on Kane's regulatory model. The model embodies an interpretative vision of cyclical interaction between political and economic processes of regulation and economic processes of regulation avoidance as opposing forces that adapt continuously to each other. The adoption between the two evolves as a series of lagged responses, with regulators and regulatees, each seeking to maximise his own objectives, conditional on how they perceive the opposing party to be behaving (Kane, p355).

This theory can be best looked at through the Hegelian process of change with three stages: thesis, antithesis, and synthesis. As such the regulator dialectic pits the regulators against the regulatees in an on-going struggle. It all starts with the regulators attempting to impose constraints on the financial system like interest rate, product or geographic controls, on the financial institutions or regulatees. The regulatees who are driven by profit or wealth maximisation motives, attempt to circumvent the restrictions because they act as taxes on their profits. If it so happens that the circumvention is successful, which usually is the case because profit-motivated individuals tend to move faster and are more efficient than bureaucrats, then the regulators attempt to close the "window" or "loophole" and the struggle becomes an on-going one (Sinkey, 1989, p.160). So there is a simultaneous resolving and renewing of an endless series of conflicts between market or economic institutions and politically imposed restraints or regulations.

The process is simplified as follows:

Regulation Imposed - Regulatory Avoidance - Regulation - Regulation Avoidance

The process continues and a stationary equilibrium is virtually impossible to achieve (Kane, op. cit.). It is this process of struggle which spurs financial innovation by regulated firms, and encourages less-regulated ones to infringe upon the more regulated firms. We see then that the regulatory dialectic can also be viewed as a theory of financial innovation.

In Kane's (ibid.) words, "A completely deregulated state," if achieved, would almost certainly contain unexploited opportunities for an individual sector to benefit from accumulating and exercising political power. This implies that the existence of regulations as restraints brings about financial innovation which allows for all opportunities that may exist in order to increase profits that could be limited by regulation.

Another writer with similar views as those of Kane is Merton H Miller. According to Miller, major impulses to successful financial innovations over the last three decades have been regulation and taxes. The tax structure both motivates and defines a successful innovation. Each innovation that does its job successfully earns an immediate reward for its adopters in the form of tax money saved. In fact, countries have to change tax systems because if they left them unchanged for generations or so, an equilibrium would emerge in which no incentive is left for shifting income from one form to another, in particular from higher taxed forms to lower-taxed ones. As such, for a variety of reasons - including the desire to blunt the force of previous successful innovations by tax payers - most governments prefer to keep changing the structure, thereby altering the internal rate differentials and creating new opportunities for financial innovation (Miller, 1986). Here again the system works like that of Kane's "regulatory dialectic".

Although Miller used tax for his example he fell short of stating that the same process can be seen at work anywhere in a financial system subject to government regulation. He concludes by pointing out that pressures to innovate around prohibited types of transactions or around newly imposed or newly-effected interest rates ceilings, are particularly strong, but even what is purported to be deregulation can trigger changes that go far beyond the intentions of the original sponsors.

Briefly, Miller says, "The major impulses to successful financial innovations have come from regulations and taxes. The outlook for the future is for a slowing down of the rate of financial innovation, but much more growth and improvement is still in prospect." Innovations can either be "transitory" or "permanent." Some financial innovation will have a period of success and disappear once a particular regulation or tax that fuelled its initial success has been removed. However a few financial innovations are non-transitory in that they survive and continue to grow even after the initiating force has been removed. These are the permanent innovations. A good example of a financial innovation induced by regulation is the Eurodollar market. It arose due to a curious restriction in the United States, known as Regulation Q. This regulation, among others, placed a ceiling on the rate of interest that commercial banks could offer on their time-deposits. During much of the period after the second World War, the rate ceiling was not critically below the market clearing level, if not actually above. However, in the latter part of the 1960s and early 1970s there were rises in US and World interest rates. It was this time that the US money market realised that restrictions of regulation Q did not apply to the dollar denominated time deposits in their overseas deposits.

Another example of an innovation due to tax here is the Eurobond market which was triggered by a 30 percent withholding tax on interest

31

payment on bonds sold in the US to overseas investors. This was in the late 1960s.

Constraint- induced innovation

The major work on constraint-induced innovation was done by William L. Silber. His hypothesis is that new financial instruments or practices are innovated to remove or reduce the financial constraints imposed on the firms. According to him, firms maximise utility subject to a number of constraints which are imposed both externally and internally. External constraints, more often than not, are government regulations. Though the market place also constrains the firms, it is clear that government regulation does indeed impose constraints and thereby induces innovation; but he goes further than that by pointing out that the behaviour of the financial firm is constrained by other factors as well, including self-imposed constraints and market imposed constraints (W L Silber, 1975, p65).

One market constraint or situation is where a financial firm has market power. It will set prices or yields and accept whatever volume of funds are offered. On the other hand, if it is a price taker, then it buys that quantity of funds that maximises its utility. It follows then that the market place generally defines the parameters of demand and supply for different financial products and simultaneously identifies the policy tools available to the firm (W. L. Silber, 1983, p89).

Constraints, which are set internally, also influence the optimisation problem. A firm may establish a target rate of growth for total assets or it may have self-imposed liquidity requirements specifying the desired percentage of the total portfolio in some particular asset. Another inherent constraint for a financial firm in its effort to maximise utility is that the sum of all assets minus liabilities and capital must be equal to zero. That is, financial firms fundamentally aim at maximising profits.

These constraints create the necessary conditions that may induce innovation. Silber's position is thus very clear. For him, optimising firms will innovate when exogenous changes alter their constraints and re-optimisation will take place having regards to the costs of developing innovations (Podoloski, p186). There are basically two types of changes that induce firms to undertake the search costs required to modify its traditional policy tools. First, exogenous changes in constraints force a reduction in the utility of the firm, and the firm innovates in an effort to return to its previous level of utility. Second, innovation responds to an increase in the cost of adhering to a constraint. The only way out of such changes is financial innovation which, of course, circumvents the constraints.

To give a better picture of his analysis W. L. Silber also looked at a number of specific constraints that cause financial innovation (W. L. Silber, 1975, p67). First, the most abrupt change faced by firms would appear to be the imposition of regulations by government or government agencies, an example being the legislation of the 1960s in the U.S.A. aimed at the banking system and financial intermediaries. Second, we know from the above that increasing costs of adhering to an existing regulatory constraint induces innovation. A good example of this is the interest-ceiling imposed on the deposits of commercial banks, which become more costly as interest rates on other financial instruments rise, hence the need for innovation. In the third place, declining demand for a particular category of a firm's assets may also prompt financial innovation. Thus, in general as the interest rate on a particular asset category declines, the labour resources administering such assets (loans) will try to maintain their sub-market for funds by altering characteristics of the asset.

Fourth, declining growth in total sources of funds may cause innovation. If the growth rate of inflow of funds falls below a minimum target growth rate, then, the firm will undertake policies to achieve its desired growth target. Once the growth rate makes the constraint optimisation unacceptable, pressures to innovate emerge. The fifth source of financial innovation, in this respect, may be the risk dimension of the firm's utility function and the stochastic nature of the constraints confronting the firm. For instance, when the market for a firm's liability changes from monopoly to perfect competition, risk-induced innovation has to take place because interest rate variability begins to affect the variance of the firm's profits. For example greater volatility and level of both interest rates and inflation during the 1960s, 1970s and 1980s imposed pressure for innovation. So competitive pressures are healthy, providing the incentive for dynamism, efficiency and innovation.

As Robin Leigh-Pemberton (1985 p13) states, "some of the changes in instruments, markets, and financial behaviour, have been primarily defensive, to allow financial intermediaries to protect both themselves, and in some cases their clients, against the worsening uncertainties and risk caused by such volatility". The more volatile the interest rate and exchange rate rises, the greater are the risks inherent in having a mismatched maturity or currency structure of assets and liability. Situations like this have led some financial intermediaries to make innovations enabling them to achieve a more closely matched book and to shift risk to those who are willing to absorb it. These may include a switch to variable rate lending, replacing fixed rate loans, and the development of instruments such as options, futures and swaps mainly used to hedge the risks and uncertainties in volatile interest rates and exchange rates.

Sinkey's model

Another author who has not remained outside the debate on what stimulates financial innovation is Joseph F. Sinkey Jr. He says that the interaction of Technology, Regulation, Interest rate, Customers (competition for), and Capital adequacy (with German spelling of capital) (TRICK) as well as rational self-interest combine to produce financial innovation. In this context self-interest simply refers to the fact that the managers of financial service firms look out for themselves (utility maximisation for themselves) and for the interest of their shareholders (Sinkey, p.203). In short the model is:

TRICK + Rational Self-interest = Financial Innovation.

For Sinkey, it is this motivation (self-interest) in conjunction with the forces of change captured by TRICK that lead to financial innovation. In other words, all financial innovations including adjustable-rate mortgages, electronic funds transfer systems (for instance automated teller machines) holding company movement, and regional interstate banking, can be explained by the above model.

It will be noted here that even Sinkey recognises the importance of the profit motive, which he has chosen to call rational self-interest, in determining or inducing financial innovation.

Transactions cost induced financial innovation

Other authors have pointed out that the reduction of transactions cost is a dominant factor in financial innovation. Basically, there are two aspects to this hypothesis. First, the reduction of transactions cost is seen as the primary motive for financial innovation. Second, innovation is essentially a response to the potential for cost reduction offered primarily by technical progress. Again the role of technology in financial innovation is emphasised here.

However this theory of financial innovation faced difficulties due to the fact that the transaction costs are not easy to define and are even more difficult to measure. Usually they are described as the costs of "going to a bank" or as broker's fees, which include a variety of costs such as direct charges for buying and selling financial assets (brokerage) on the cost of transferring the title to ownership between contracting parties. Problems of definition makes economists leave out transaction costs in empirical studies (Podoloski, p.203).

Evidence

A number of empirical studies have indicated that financial innovation is constraint induced. For the period 1952 to 1970 the constraint induced model was successfully explained using new bank products as observations. For the observation period 1970 to 1982 the model explained about 60 per cent of the financial innovations (W. L. Silber, p94). In another study by W. L. Silber in 1983, which was basically a check-list of "exogenous causes" of 38 financial innovation in the USA during the period 1970-1982, he found out that the main potential causes of innovations are inflation, volatility of interest rates, technology, regulatory changes, and internationalisation (Podoloski, p204). Despite the evidence, specific predictions of financial innovations are by no means easy.

Financial innovation and reform in Zambia

The financial system in Zambia has followed the traditional path of financially repressed systems throughout the 60s, 70s, and the 80s. The salient features of a financially repressed system were very evident in the strict controls (ceilings) on interest rates by the Bank of Zambia until 1992, massive controls of the foreign exchange market (through exchange control regulations which were abolished in early 1994), concentration of commercial banks (only 4 to 5) until the late 1980s, directed credit portfolios for lending institutions and the predominance of the curb market for both money markets ad foreign exchange.

However, the 1990s brought a new dawn on the horizon. A new government came to power through the October 31, 1991 multi-party elections. With it came a completely different approach and orientation to the financial sector. It committed itself to reforming the financial system through liberalising it as much as possible. In line with this policy, we have seen drastic changes in the financial services industry. To start with, it is a policy which began during the Second Republic and has been enhanced with the advent of the Third Republic. This is the opening-up of the banking industry and financial services industry in general. As a result, the number of banks and financial institutions has since ballooned, and more have been registered and are expected to be operational in the near future. Even the insurance business is no longer the domain (monopoly) of the Zambia State Insurance Corporation. What a relief! There are now six insurance companies with more expected to be established in the near future.

Late 1992 saw another major departure from the traditional administration of the financial system in Zambia. The Bureau de Change System of determining the exchange rate was introduced. The exchange rate was to be determined by the market forces of demand and supply, and any company can buy and sell foreign exchange from the public by way of establishing a Bureau de Change following the regulations given by the Bank of Zambia. This put paid to an archaic foreign exchange regulatory system with rigorous regulations which neither allocated foreign exchange nor determined the exchange rate efficiently. Because of the new system, stability of the foreign exchange market does not seem to be too far off.

During the same year, interest rate determination was liberalised. In other words, ceilings were abolished. An opportunity was created for the banks to price the services according to their risks and on the basis of the expected returns. The previous system allowed the lending institutions to rely on non-price factors in distinguishing "bad borrowers" from "good borrowers" thereby denying the most productive projects credit, especially the small-scale industries.

The treasury bill market was also introduced and was quite active in 1993 and has continued to be an attractive asset for both those in the financial services industry and the firms in the other types of businesses. This is true for both corporations and individuals.

The year 1994 was greeted by the abolition of the Exchange Control Act thereby paving way to the opening of foreign currency accounts, a thing one could hardly dream about a few years ago.

Another very important event for the Zambian financial system has been the establishment of the Lusaka Stock Exchange which started operations in

February, 1994. This has almost completed the major requirements of a liberalised financial market.

Apart from the specific changes referred to above, other factors have also changed in a manner which could provide the enabling environment to encourage financial institutions to innovate. Some of these include changes in tax, competition, technology, volatile inflation, interest and exchange rates, and market inefficiencies.

The changes enumerated above in money, capital, foreign exchange markets, insurance industry and others have created the necessary atmosphere for dynamic and proactive financial institutions to innovate. Every new system usually has a lot of openings for the attentive and outward looking bankers and financial experts to innovate. They will take advantage of the weak and learning regulatory system to make the best returns before the regulatory authority identifies the loopholes, and puts in regulations to close them up.

Some of the innovations we have seen recently include: (1) introduction of bank accounts which have characteristics of current and savings accounts (e.g. Zanaco Saver's account) which allow customers to deposit money as savings and at the same time provide a cheque book; (2) Savings accounts which include the facility of a cheque book; (3) Computerisation of most bank operations or information system (e.g. Barclays Bank of Zambia, Standard Chartered Bank, and Zambia National Commercial Bank); and (4) Introduction of electronic technology using Automatic Teller Machines (e.g. Zanaco 24 Hours account currently offered in Lusaka and Ndola only). With the prevailing financial environment, we should see more and more financial innovations on the market.

However, the liberalised financial sector has not come with "goodies" only; in fact, it presents more challenges to the management of financial institutions and their supervision. Within the few years of financial liberalisation, the country has seen the collapse of three indigenous banks, namely; Meridien BIAO Bank (which was the fourth largest bank in the country at the time of its demise in 1995), African Commercial Bank (ACB), and Commerce Bank. In addition to these bank failures, the Co-operative Bank has also failed to continue operations.

The major reason that is cited for the failure of the banks is poor management in a competitive environment in general and specific issues such as lending too much money to some directors, and/or over-exposure of the banks by lending a large proportion of the bank's assets to the same group of companies (as was the case for ACB). Financial innovation could also explain some of the bank failures. For instance, Meridien BIAO Bank was a leader in financial innovation after the liberalisation of the sector. It was the first to introduce plastic money in Zambia through its Meridien Card.

Conclusion

This paper has carried out a survey of various theories that attempt to explain why financial innovation takes place. It should be noted that Kane's theory which is based on the "regulatory dialectic" is insufficient. Of course we do not doubt the fact that regulations play an important role but the perspective that it is the only explanation for financial innovation is rather too narrow to be applicable to a number of innovations. For instance, Scotland had no regulations affecting banks and had no central bank until 1845 and yet the period prior to this year saw a number of financial innovations, such as the "cash credit"; branch banking; the payment of interest on deposits; and the provision of various borrowing schemes (Johnson, 1988, p.2). We are therefore left with no option except to say that regulation, on its own, is not an adequate explanation. In any case, we are aware that some financial innovations are due to circumvention of regulations as Kane rightly stated, but it is just one element of a more general category of innovation generating phenomena.

Although Schumpeter's theory gives us some insight, it does not really deal with financial innovation in particular. His theory basically links financial change with technological and institutional development in the real sector. This could be true. But it is not supported by the fact that there have been financial innovations since the 1970s which have occurred with a background of a generally depressed economic atmosphere, but in an environment of structural and technological change, inflation, and deregulation (Podoloski, p185).

Sinkey's model is an interesting one in that it covers quite a large spectrum of a financial firm's activity and its environment but it falls short of covering all the possible variables. The transactions cost hypothesis is also too narrow to explain a sizeable number of innovations.

In our pursuit to find a theory that explains financial innovation, we are seeking one that would cover almost all variables which induce financial innovation. It must be generally applicable to any situation without exception. Of all the theories discussed above, Silber's constraint-induced financial innovation theory provides the most reasonable, general explanation. Almost every situation we can think of, where financial innovation takes place, there is at least some kind of constraint which can not be eliminated without innovation.

Constraint-induced innovation theory, in fact, covers all the other explanations. There is, more often than not, a constraint of some kind to circumvent or beat. It may be external, internal or indeed self-imposed. The major constraints that will induce or prompt financial innovation include:

(1) volatile inflation, interest, and exchange rates;
(2) regulatory changes and circumvention of regulations;
(3) tax changes;
(4) level of economic activity;
(5) communications and technology;
(6) market inefficiencies;
(7) the pattern of net flows of international savings and investment (as reflected by current account imbalances); and
(8) competition.

It is generally agreed that these factors are very influential, though there may be some disagreement as to their relative importance (Van Horne, 1985 and BSI, 1986).

However all the constraints above have some connection of some sort to profit maximisation which is the basic objective of every business concern. In other words, utility maximisation is at the heart of every innovation (or underlies every innovation).

But what are the major benefits of innovations? Innovations in financial institutions and practices improve the ability to bear risk (e.g. in futures markets), lower transactions cost (automated teller machines), and circumvents outmoded regulations (money market mutual funds, regulation Q). In conclusion, financial innovation yields economic benefits that are no less real than physical technology. From the above discussion we can safely conclude that all financial innovations are constraint -induced.

It is needless here to say that the reforms that are going on in the financial system in Zambia today provide a rare opportunity for those in the financial services industry to invent and innovate through offering new products (services), new methods of providing the same products, reducing transactions costs, reducing their customers' waiting time in banks, opening new markets, and winning or attracting new clients. Those institutions that do not take advantage of the current changes will have only themselves to blame if the values of their institutions plummet over the next few years. The current competitive pressures are healthy and provide the incentive for dynamism, efficiency and innovation.

Bibliography

Bank for International Settlements (1986), *Recent Innovations in International Banking*, BIS: Basle.

Johnson, L.T. (1988), *The Theory of Financial Innovation*: A New Approach, Institute of European Finance: Bangor.

Kane, E. J. (1981), 'Accelerating Inflation, Technological Innovations and the Decreasing Effectiveness of Banking Regulation', *Journal of Finance*, May.

Leigh-Pemberton, R. (1985), 'Shifting Frontiers in Financial Markets: Their causes and Consequences', *Bank of England Quarterly Bulletin*, June.

Miller, M.H.(1986), 'Financial Innovation: The Last Twenty Years and the Next', *Revue de la Banque*, Number 7.

Podoloski, T.M. (1986), *Financial Innovation and Money Supply*, Basil Blackwell limited, Oxford.

Silber, W.L. (ed.) (1975), *Financial Innovation*, D.C. Heath and Company, Lexington.

Silber, W,L., (1983), 'The Process of Financial Innovation', *American Economic Review*, May.

Sinkey, J. F., Jr. (1989), *Commercial Bank Financial Management in the Financial Services Industry*, 3rd edition, Macmillan published company, New York.

Van Horne, J.C. (1985), 'Of Financial Innovations and Excess', *Journal of Finance*, July.

4 Land tenure and economic development in Zambia

Amos Kambenja

Introduction

One of the crucial problems facing the third world countries in recent years is the existence of a widespread under-nourishment and poverty. In a report about African food requirements in 1991, the Director General of Food and Agricultural Organisation (FAO) Edouard Saouma mentioned that there is a widening gap between the need and the food available in Africa. He warned that unless there was massive acceleration of the flow of food aid to the affected population, the world was likely to experience widespread deaths from starvation (Svedber, p1991: 158).

A study conducted in some rural areas of Zambia in 1991 revealed that six in ten children are undernourished and that one in twenty is severely malnourished. In fact, malnutrition was reported to be one of the major public health problems in Zambia (Times of Zambia, June 20, 1991).

The challenge of raising the level of economic well-being of developing countries including Zambia is, therefore, well known. It is generally recognised that increasing the productivity of these countries' agriculture is essential to their economic development. In other words, the land tenure system which may have an observable effect on the agricultural productivity, determines the pace of economic development for many poor countries.

Economic development is perceived in this paper to encompass increased investment, enlarged markets of agricultural produce and inputs; reduction in unemployment, mass poverty and social inequality. It is also the perception of this paper that economic development is accompanied by a rapid increase

42

in demand for agricultural products and that failure to expand food supplies in line with growth in demand can seriously impede economic growth.

Land tenure is perceived in this paper to mean a developmental institution that embodies legal contractual or customary arrangements whereby people in farming gain access to productive opportunities on the land. In short, land tenure institutions attempt to shape the pattern of income distribution in farming sector (Dorner P. 1972: 51).

The land tenure institutions help to determine who shall farm, how much land, and how much income the individual farmer or a group of farmers can earn from farming. Although they are important in food and agricultural production, land tenure systems do not exist in isolation. They are linked closely to the requirement of labour, capital, and product markets in ensuring the future security of farming opportunities (La-Anyane, S. 1985: 45). The viability of any land tenure system can, therefore, be best judged on the grounds of the existing system of organisation in agriculture; and prevailing economic, institutional and technological conditions in the society; and the stage of economic development and industrialisation of the community.

Systems of agricultural land tenure are quite complex and diverse. For simplicity, we make a broad distinction between modern and traditional tenure system. Under a modern capitalist model, land ownership is private. Landowners make decisions about acquisition, use and disposal of their land, subject only to the laws of the land. With a modern socialist model, land is owned by the state, although the responsibility for cultivation is often given to co-operative groups or collectives. The collective farmers are required to meet production norms and delivery quotas set by the state.

Under traditional systems the ownership of land may be either communal or private. Under communal or tribal ownership, farmers have individual right of cultivation, but not necessarily that of exclusive use of the land. For instance, grazing rights are often held in common. Under private ownership, the rights of ownership and cultivation may either be exercised by the same person (i.e. the owner-farmer); or separately by landlords and tenants respectively. In the traditional model, the landlord - tenant relationship has generally been feudal in character with tenants paying and landlords receiving rent in the form of either a share of the crop or provision labour services (Ghatak, S. & Ingersent, K. 1984: 238).

Land tenure and property rights

Land tenure arrangements are of special significance to crop production in Zambia because they define people's access to resources and income earning opportunities. They are directly associated with income distribution in rural areas. In Zambia there exists two forms of land tenure, one is customary and the other is statutory, i.e. based on legal principles.

Statutory tenure

The land reform measures which were proclaimed by way of a presidential decree in 1975, and which were subsequently backed up by legislation, abolished all freehold titles and reduced all longer leases to statutory leases of 99 years.

The Land (Conversion of Titles) Act No. 20 of 1975, also vested all land in the President of the country who is to hold it in perpetuity in trust on behalf of the people of Zambia (Cap. 289).

Statutory land tenure in Zambia is a reconciliation of private property and state property. All interests individuals hold are derived from that of the President as the principal land holder. However, the state as the landlord has offered the tenant the freedom to use his land subject only to the town and country planning restrictions and compulsory purchase orders. Unlike the English-type landlord and tenant relationship where the obligations of reciprocal covenants or contractual terms are agreed upon between private parties, in Zambia covenants are statutory. They are designed by the government to protect the interests of the government as the landlord and the lessee as the tenant.

In Zambia, less than 10% of interests in land are held under statutory tenure, while the rest of the land inhabited by the country's peasant population, is held under customary or traditional tenure. Since it is in customary land where poverty and hunger are on the increase and where the lives of the people need to be ameliorated through the restructuring of the developmental institutions, the emphasis in this paper is placed on traditional or customary land tenure.

Traditional tenure

The traditional land system is inherent in the culture, customs and practices of the people, and is passed from generation to generation through an unwritten law. Although the use of land is individualistic; (i.e. a person is free to use land either for cultivation or for housing with no interference from other community members), there are certain uses which are communal, and these may include grazing of animals after harvesting of crops, collection of firewood and wild fruits, etc. Any member of the community can enter any land without crops to collect any natural resource with no hindrance by other community members (Mvunga, 1980:23).

In most parts of Zambia (except for the Western Province), land is allodial, i.e. the principal holder is non-existent. Land is owned by the community as a whole, with the chief or the village headman assuming the role of controller of the use and allocation of land.

The perception of ownership by the community as a group gives rise to a number of issues: If you have to belong to the community group to have rights over land, then it follows that you cannot sell it individually for value. If you did, it is likely that ownership will pass out of the hands of the group. In any case, research by Mvunga, (1980) discovered that land *per se* is not traditionally regarded as having intrinsic value, but only value emanating from its ability to produce food. Thus, the idea of sale of land is also alien. It then follows that if you cannot sell or otherwise transfer land except within your group, you cannot, therefore, mortgage it. If you cannot mortgage it, you cannot raise long-term finance and can, therefore, hardly develop it beyond subsistence level.

In areas under the traditional land tenure system, the emphasis is placed on equality of opportunity; i.e. access to land for all on which to grow food for oneself and close family relations. Land creates social and cultural bonds amongst community members. Any changes in the form of ownership will, therefore, constitute changes in the socio-economic pattern of the society, and this entails changes in the society itself.

Besides the social bonds that keep the community members together, customary land tenure has been associated with various economic and environmental problems.

45

Problems of customary land tenure

Problems of the customary land tenure are many and varied. In Zambia the most common include:

Tribalism resulting in mal-distribution of land Land under the jurisdiction of one tribe may be overcrowded, arid or semi-arid, where food production is risky, while good potential land in the jurisdiction of a neighbouring tribe lies idle or is under-utilised. Citizens in need of land for farming do not have equal opportunities and rights of access to these under-utilised lands.

Absence of land planning This has resulted in wrong setting of farm holdings likely to cause soil erosion and to create inconveniently shaped holdings for successful farming operations. Processes leading to soil loss and degradation in rural Zambia are basically the result of inappropriate farming practices which are brought about by increased food demand by the rapidly increasing human population, and require education in land use planning. Sadly, allocations of land by traditional chiefs or community elders are usually not effectively controlled by the government agencies. The Department of National Resources, whose duties include the control of land utilisation in traditional lands has no human, material and financial resources to effectively carry out its responsibilities.

Insecurity of tenure is another feature of customary land ownership which has been identified as causing developmental problems. This oft-talked about feature is, however, not treated with much importance as many other authors have done for reasons further detailed below:

Using Acquaye's words, the debilitating effect of the customary land tenure on agricultural development has been pronounced by commentators so frequently and so loudly that it now tends to be accepted as a universal and incontrovertible fact - almost as an article of faith (Acquaye, E. & Crocombe, R 1984: 19). One of the reasons advanced against the customary land tenure system is that it provides inadequate security of tenure and consequently, the incentive for investment in agriculture. It is also believed that customary land tenure impedes the development of an active market in land, and that it discourages the extension of credit (ibid., Aquaye, E. & Crocombe, R 1984:19). Recent empirical studies, however, are dispelling such beliefs.

Evidence gathered by Migot-Adholla and other World Bank researchers in a cross-sectional study in Kenya, Rwanda and Ghana, between 1987-88 revealed no relationship between security of tenure and agricultural productivity. They discovered that without accompanying improvements in infrastructure, price incentives, credit facilities, marketing services, and technology, any type of land tenure will not be able to induce agricultural development (Migot-Adholla, S. et al ,1991).

This proposition, however, is difficult to substantiate because it relates to factors that support land tenure and not land tenure *per se*. In other words, the defects are not caused by the land tenure. It was stated above that the tenure alone cannot bring about economic development unless supplemented by supportive institutions such as marketing, credit supply, extension service, and infrastructure provision, etc. and if empirical studies have proved that without these supportive institutions, any form of tenure will not be able to induce agricultural development, then it is these institutions that need to be improved and not the land tenure.

In Zambia, the economic under-development in rural areas appears to be mainly caused by factors other than security of land tenure for the following reasons:

First, the state credit institutions in Zambia were only able to provide credit to about 50% of the applicants between 1980 and 1984 (GRZ, Evaluation of the performance of Zambia's Maize sub-Sector, 1990:65). Second, every year food is reported to go to waste in some rural areas, either at the depots or in the fields due to poor storage facilities and inadequate processing industries, as well as lack of speedy and efficient transport.

Third, the parastatal companies established by the Government are hardly involved in the marketing of traditional food crops such as cassava, sorghum, millet and sweet potatoes, possibly due to lack of roads leading to production areas, and organised collection points. Fourth, even in maize growing areas, input supply points are usually located several kilometres away, beyond the reach of most peasants whose only means of transport are either bicycles or ox-drawn carts. In such circumstances, therefore, blaming security of land tenure for the rural poverty is running away from the cardinal developmental issues.

Security of tenure is necessary only if a motivated and business-minded farmer intends to use the title deed of a marketable piece of land as collateral against a loan (where it is easily obtainable). Security of tenure is not necessary in a remote customary land area where demand for land is non-existent. Consequently, talking about security of tenure as a means of upgrading lives of people in traditional lands is a fallacy.

The views on security of tenure discussed above do not, however, dispel the developmental problems of land under customary ownership. Distribution and land use planning and management problems still pose a serious concern to land development. These must be tackled urgently if Zambia's land assets are to be put to their optimum use and if all citizens are to be afforded fair access to and rights in land.

The question, however, remains that of the appropriate policy measures that must be put in place to ameliorate developmental problems caused by the customary land tenure systems in Zambia.

There appears to be a great difficulty of determining the appropriate system of agricultural development. One of the problems is that of balancing social equality and economic efficiency. For example, the fixing of a twenty acre ceiling on land ownership in India might have fulfilled an egalitarian motive of enabling every farming household in the country to have a minimum subsistence plot, but this may not be followed by the generation of surplus food for export. Some people who despise manual labour may keep land idle for prestige rather than putting it to productive use. in addition, the provision of inputs, marketing services and infrastructure may be too erratic to permit high productivity.

The second difficulty is that of determining the most suitable system of tenure on the basis of comparison. This is so because every society is different from others, and it does not follow that a system that is working well in one country will necessarily work well in another country. For example, collective or village farms are working well in China, but not in Tanzania. The third difficulty is that of determining the appropriateness of a system in terms of the "cost-benefit" ratio, i.e. the capital expended on a particular programme may not be recoverable.

The policy strategies to be used to improve the lives of the people in traditional lands will mainly depend on the political ideology of the country at the time of tackling the problem. The two well-known models used in the Eastern and Southern African region based on different ideologies are the Kenyan and the Tanzanian models. We discuss these in greater detail below.

The Tanzanian model

The Arusha Declaration of 5th February 1967 declared categorically, that Tanzania intended to be a socialist state and incorporated the main principles that no man should exploit another and that development must be based on the people's own work - in short, equality and self-reliance (Mkatte, 1983).

Tanzania is, therefore, following a model of group farming-based on collective ownership and exploitation of land by (Ujamaa) village communities. Land tenure is based on block farm plots, which are larger than the homestead plots and communal farms. Proceeds from the farms are used for the development of communal facilities; Part of these proceeds is stored and the remainder is distributed to each community member according to his work (Laurence, J.C.D. 1976).

Problems encountered in the implementation of Ujamaa were reported by Mkatte to include, lack of knowledge of human settlement issues on the part of the implementers which led to poor settlement site selection, and lack of knowledge and data on soil characteristics, land carrying capacity and suitability of vegetation for domestic animals. The Ujamaa policy was, however, a great step towards rural development by way of customary land tenure adjustments.

The present general land policy for Zambia is that of liberalisation of the land market and the non-interference by government in matters of land transactions, though the government has rejected the re-introduction of freehold ownership of land tenure with a view to controlling development. Inspite of similarities in clauses, statutory covenants and conditions, it is unlikely that the Zambian government would embrace the Tanzanian model. This is so because the Tanzanian model is equality-based, and Zambia which has already declared the adoption of neo-classical efficiency-based models in its economic development would more likely avoid this pattern of development.

Kenyan model

Plans to improve rural land in Kenya started with the introduction of the Colonial Development and Welfare Acts of 1940 and 1945 and the large sums of development funds pledged by the British Government during the same period.

After protracted debates and consultations between government authorities and the notable African elders, it was decided in 1949 that some modern form of tenure should be introduced to remove any fears that existed among African landowners and to give them a feeling of complete security. It was also believed that the security of tenure that would be provided by the Title Deed would encourage better farming methods and avoid fragmentation of highly populated Kikuyu land in the Central Province (Sorrenson, 1967:63). Some government officials in 1950 were of the opinion that if the aim of the government was to issue and register private titles and if land was to provide security for agricultural credit, then there was no alternative to the imposition of English Land Law, or, better still a modified version thereof.

To implement the above mentioned policies, the government with advice from Swynnerton R.J.M. and others tried the processes of sporadic consolidation of land parcels in Central Province. This was later followed by settlement and adjudication of titles to the settlers on freehold basis.

Freehold titles of individual family farms, therefore, is the dominant development policy in most rural areas of Kenya. This was achieved through the introduction of several types of settlement programmes, namely: Million-Acre (or Conventional) Settlement Programme in 1961; Shirika Settlement Programme in 1971; and Harambee Settlement Programme in 1969. Others are Haraka Settlement Programme in 1965 and the more recent State Land Settlement Programme in the Coast Province in Lamu and Kalifi Districts.

The Kenyan model of private family farms as a strategy of rural development is indeed in line with Zambia's rural development concepts. The only difference is that in Kenya there are freehold land interests whereas in Zambia, land tenure interests are limited to statutory leases of 99 years.

The question is: can Zambia adopt the same model during this era considering the present economic situation?

Kenya succeeded in its programmes at the time when the general economic conditions were favourable. The quality and quantity of its staff involved in the implementation of rural settlement programmes were good. For instance, in December, 1975, the Kenyan Department of Settlement had an establishment of 1.306 posts. Half of its 48 senior positions were filled by people holding either degrees or diplomas in fields relevant to agriculture and land settlement (Departmental Annual Report, 1975). Furthermore, only about 20% of land in Kenya is arable (UNICEF Report (Draft) 1991: 8). This implied that the development effort was, therefore, manifesting in areas of high level of marketability in land, inputs and crops. All these factors are not comparable to Zambia's present situation with most of its fertile lands located in sparsely populated, arid and semi-arid areas. It is unlikely, therefore, that Zambia can easily resolve its rural development problems using the Kenyan model.

Government view on land tenure and economic development

The Movement for Multiparty Democracy (MMD) and its Manifesto Provisions on Land Law and Policy Reforms for the Zambian Third Republican Government has put in place fundamental land development policies that are outlined more fully below:

The MMD Government recognises the need to approach the land reform issue with a sense of calculated urgency as land was central to any development efforts. For this reason, the Government is now set to liberalise the land and property market since they know that development of land costs money, and that it is fundamentally wrong for any responsible government to give land freely as was the case in the past (Mushota, 1993: 38). However, the Government has proposed to enact a new law that will ensure that the majority of title deeds are given to small scale farmers and other native entrepreneurs and that the big investors, both foreign and local, do not marginalise the poor and other vulnerable groups of the society, with impunity or otherwise. The Government does not want to see a situation develop where only 5% or less, of the population of Zambia owned all the land. Relative equity will have to prevail in all processes of land identification and allocation. In other words, the thinking behind the MMD land policy is that the investor's money is not everything (ibid. Mushota, 1993: 40).

The reforms would ensure a way of recognising indigenous people's rights on already settled land currently designated as 'customary' - that is, in the event of granting individual title deeds, no forced resettlement or removal of people on that land should be permissible. Statutory leasehold tenure of 99 years is the adopted government policy, and it is to be made uniform in both traditional and state lands.

The Government also proposes to make traditional land more marketable than before. However, no economic measures are given to make traditional land marketable. The Government has also observed that communal ownership of land lacked incentives for land preservation and often led to land degradation. It is for this reason that the Government strongly emphasises that caution ought to be exercised in issuing title deeds to indigenous people and in selling land, though no modality on land allocation was given to avoid degradation.

The Government further recognises that traditional chiefs hold land as trustees on behalf of not only the dead who are buried on that land, but also on behalf of the present and future generations. This creates fears in the chiefs that granting of title deeds would entail the loss of their authority over land and their subjects. No clear policy is, however, in existence to deal with this fear, apart from the unproven sentiments that 90% of chiefs are willing to give title and that 70% of the applications for title deeds are for customary land (ibid. Mushota: 43). These applications may, however, not have been lodged by peasants but by urban dwellers who intended to acquire land in their areas of origin.

The above outline of policies on land tenure and reform suggests that the Zambian government intends to follow the "price and marketing model" in its effort to improve development in rural areas. The model calls for government policy interventions into outcomes in domestic markets, but uses markets and the private marketing sector as the vehicle for those policy interventions (Timmer, P.C., 1988: 326). The model falls within the purview of the neo-classical welfare economics where the rational individual is deemed the best judge of his own welfare, with marginal public participation.

There is recognition in this model of widespread market failures in agriculture as well as extensive Government failures in the implementation of direct economic functions (ibid. Timmer, 1988: 326).

Inputs in this model suggest changes in the system of land tenure. Although, as already mentioned, empirical studies in Ghana, Kenya and Rwanda by the World Bank showed no relationship between land tenure and agricultural growth. Other inputs in the model include the efficient service institutions of farm input and crop marketing, processing, credit supply, and an efficient extension service to disseminate information to farmers on the use of fertilisers, scientific and technological innovations, storage methods and so on. Local government services are required in the development of feeder roads, and irrigation projects. Physical inputs of new and improved farms, such as new crop varieties, fertilisers, insecticides and herbicides are also part of the inputs of the model.

Conclusion

Rural development policies recently introduced in Zambia to upgrade the standards of living in traditional land are welcome. In fact, these same policies are being applied fruitfully in other countries in the region such as Zimbabwe, Malawi, Kenya and South Africa. However, the input of this development model requires adequate finance and qualified manpower. The model should also prevail in an environment where the farmer, and not the government, is the decision maker; where prices of agricultural produce are flexible and reflecting the supply and demand conditions in the local and world markets; where all categories of farmers are accorded equal opportunities of selling their produce; where credit is supplied to all capable and credit-worthy farmers on equal terms; and where land titles are issued only to motivated and productive farmers.

The government should, therefore, study and strengthen the land administration capacity of communal land tenure systems possibly by giving local leaders additional powers to administer the allocation and management of land parcels. The government should also assess whether or not the current system of conversion from traditional land to state land provides adequate protection to communal land holders while at the same time providing a fair and rapid system of conversion for title seekers in the presence of cheaper and faster surveying methods.

Wholesome reform of say expropriation and distribution of land or change of tenancy may not only be unnecessary but also un-affordable to this country. This ambitious programme may not even yield economic growth and development if it is not backed by improvements in the marketing system input and crops; efficient and well organised credit and extension services and the provision of rural infrastructure.,

Change of tenancy should be directed to those areas with high population densities and where there is marketability in land. In most rural areas of the country customary collective rights need to be protected especially where these have proved to be flexible in the face of changing social and environmental circumstances.

Bibliography

Acquaye, E. and Crocombe, R. (1984), *Land Tenure and Rural Productivity in the Pacific Islands*, the University of South Pacific, Suva, Fiji.

Binswanger, Hans P., Deininger K. and Feder, G. (1993), 'Popwe, Distortions, Revolt and Reform in Agricultural and Land Relations,' paper prepared for the *Handbook of Development Economics*, Vol. III, Jere Behrman and T.N. Srinivasan, (eds).

Dorner P. (1972), *Land Reform and Economic Development*, Penguin Books Ltd, England.

Dorner, P. (1972), *Land Reform in Latin America, Issues and Cases*, Land Tenure Centre, New York.

Ghatak, S. and Ingersent, K. (1984), *Agriculture and Economic Development*, Harvester Press, London.

Kambenja, A. (1990), *Land Resettlement Programmes in Kenya, Zimbabwe and Zambia*, A Comparative Study, (Unpublished).

Kambenja, A, (1992), *Institutional Transformation of Agricultural Development*, (Unpublished Masters Thesis).

Kenya, Republic of, (1991), *National Report to the United Nations Conference on Environment and Development* (Provisional Draft).

Kenya, Republic of, (1975, 1980, 1988), *Department of Settlement, Annual Reports*, Government Printer, Nairobi.

King, R. (1977), *Land Reform - World Survey*, Bell and Sons Ltd., London.

La-Anyane, S., *Economics of Agricultural Development in Tropical Africa,* John Wiley and Sons, Chichester, New York.

Mkatte, J.J. (1983), *Land Policies and the Development of Resources: The Tanzanian Experience* (Unpublished).

Mushota, K. Remmy Kabanda, (1993), 'The MMD and Its Manifesto Provisions on Land Law and Policy Reforms for the Zambian Third Republican Government' (Unpublished).

Mvunga, M.P., (1982), *Land Law and Policy in Zambia*, University of Zambia, Institute for African Studies, Lusaka.

Sorrension, M.P.K. (1967), *Land Reform in the Kikuyu Country*, Oxford University Press, England.

Svedberg, P. (1991), Undernutrition in Sub-Saharan Africa, in Dreze, J. and Sen, A. (eds.), *The Political Economy of Hunger*, Clarendon Press, Oxford.

Times of Zambia, June 1991.

Timmer, P.C. (1988), 'Agricultural Transformation', in Chenery, H. and Srinivasan, T.N. (eds.), *Handbook of Development Economics*, Vol. 1, Elsevier Science Publishing Co., Oxford.

Warriner, D., (1969), *Land Reform in Principle and Practice*, Clarendon Press, Oxford.

World Bank, (1989), *Sub-Saharan Africa: From Crisis to Sustainable Growth* (a long term perspective study), Washington D.C. p.89.

5 Some critical issues in land policy formulation in Zambia

Moses Kaunda

Introduction

Since the advent of the Third Republic in November, 1991, the need to re-examine the established customs, institutions and practices relating to land as well as other basic tenets of land policy as formulated in the first two Republics (1964 - 1973 and 1973 - 1991) has been increasingly appreciated by pertinent professional bodies and even by the government. Thus, the Surveyors Institute of Zambia (SIZ) on November 22, 1991 held a seminar under the theme Land Development Policies - the Need for Change. As if not to be outdone, the Law Association of Zambia (LAZ) also preceded their 1992 Annual General Meeting (AGM) on 28 February with a seminar under the heading Land Law in the third Republic. More importantly, a National Conference on Land Policy and Legal Reform was organised for the period 19 July - 23 July, 1993.

The two major political parties, the ruling Movement for Multi-party Democracy (MMD) and the official opposition in Parliament, the United

National Independence Party (UNIP) have also found the area of land policy a fertile one for ideological battles. This can be illustrated by the Budget Speech, in which the Minister of Finance portrayed the current legal status of land as a major impediment to new investment; and he implicitly supported freehold tenure. Further, the Minister alluded to draft laws which would allow the valuation of land, free transfer and subdivision of land under statutory leasehold and reduction of property transfer tax.

In its reaction, UNIP opposed reintroduction of freehold system of land tenure which, it claimed, was bound to produce the kind of peasant dispossession and consequent strife witnessed in Mexico. UNIP further observed, in favour of leasehold tenure, that the Chinese 99 year lease of Hong Kong to Britain did not discourage investment, and proceeded to demand a national referendum on the question of reversion to freehold.

'Land policy' - The problem of definition

There is a general dearth of attempts at defining the phrase 'Land Policy'. Articles and books with this phrase in their titles have tended to omit any definition. Certain authors have offered two reasons to account for the lack of a concise definition: Firstly, the fact that many wide and varied topics are covered under the phrase, including those which go beyond the focus of land, such as urban government structure and finance, local and central government relations, housing and regional development policies and urban planning control: Secondly, the identification of land policy with all government guidelines concerned with land, simply because it is the government which introduces and implements these.

It is then clear, that the lack of a terse and comprehensive definition is due to the fact that, as a province of academic study, land policy does not fall exclusively within any one of the established disciplines concerned with land.

Nevertheless, the very absence of a concise definition combined with the possibility of many definitions have been offered as compelling reasons for authors to state their own understanding of 'land policy' whenever they use the phrase. (Lichfield and Darin - Drabkim, 1980: 10). We heed this counsel below.

'Land Policy' as used in this article is intended to mean 'the policy of government regarding the ownership, allocation, use (including development) and transfer of land.' As such, our understanding approximates to the conceptualisation advanced by Acquaye (1984: 24) when he postulated thus:

> Land Policy consists of the whole complex of social-economic and legal philosophies and prescriptions which govern the ownership and use of land resources in any society.

Presented in schematic form, the issues and questions involved in land policy formulation will emerge as shown in figure 1.

The Setting

Categories/status of land

By the time Zambia attained independence on 24 October, 1964, her land had been demarcated into three categories currently known as Reserves, Trust Land and State Land (Mvunga, 1980).

The said demarcation followed a policy of land reservation pursued by the colonial government of Northern Rhodesia. Under this policy, Native Reserves were set apart "for the sole and exclusive use of the natives of Northern Rhodesia" (Art. 6, the Northern Rhodesia (Crown Land and Natives Reserves) Order-in-Council, 1928), so that non-natives could acquire only limited interests in reserved land. Native Trust Land was set aside "for the use of common benefit, direct or indirect, of the natives" (Art 4(1), the Native Trust Land Order-in-Council, 1947), but non-natives could acquire more lasting interests in this category of land. They could be granted 'Rights of Occupancy' for terms not exceeding 99 years if, on the determination of the Governor, that was in general interest of the community as a whole *(Art. 5(1) (b) & 5(6))*. Crown Land was, on the other hand, intended for European occupation and use.

Critical questions
1.   Who should own and control land?

2.   Precisely what interests in land should be granted?

3.   How is the land to be allocated?

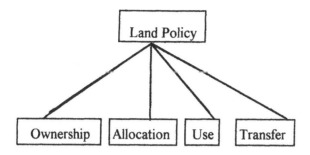

Figure 1: 'Land Policy' - the problem of definition

4.   Who should use land and how is it to be used?

5.   What other rights and obligations should be associated with land ownership?

6.   What should be the role of government in the land market?

By 1947, therefore, a spatial plan for the development of Northern Rhodesia partly as a settler colony was completed; based upon a degree of racial segregation. Three categories of land had been established and their occupation and use was principally on racial grounds, though in respect of Crown Land this was not written into Law (Government of the Republic of Zambia (GRZ), Land Commission, 1967:1).

On independence Zambia inherited the three categories of land. But colour was no longer considered paramount in allocation of land and people of all colour shades can now acquire land in any one of the three categories - which still legally exist.

The regimes of land law

Customary law   Despite the absence of specific statutory provision on the type of law to regulate land relations in Reserves and Trust Land, the practice shows that customary law does this.

The juridical basis for the application of customary law lies in its recognition by statutory law. To date, statutory law 'permits' customary law to regulate many aspects of native life. Thus, in civil cases between Africans, and particularly those relating to tenure, magistrates tend to observe and to enforce the observance of customary law subject to the 'Repugnance' and 'Incompatibility' tests; that is, so long as a particular rule of customary law is not repugnant to justice, equity or good conscience and is not incompatible either in terms of, or by necessary implication with, any written law for the time being in force in Zambia *(S.16, the Subordinate Courts Act, Cap. 45)*. Further, the High Court also has jurisdiction to enforce rules of customary law whose existence is proved to its satisfaction *(S.34(1), the High Court Act, Cap. 50)*.

Statute law   This principally regulates land rights in State Land.   It consists of the imported English law as modified, from time to time, by local enactments.

Since 1975 when the *Land (Conversion of Titles) Act, No. 20* converted all freehold interests as well as leases extending beyond one hundred years from 1 July, 1975 to statutory leases **(S.5)** the greatest interests in land that government presently grants are leases of 99 year duration.   But the following other interests: 99 year Council leases - under the *Housing (Statutory and Improvement Areas) Act, 1994*; 30 year Agricultural Leases - under the *Agricultural Lands Act. 1960*; 99 Year Reserve Leases, 33 years Reserve Leases and 5 Year Reserve Leases - under *the Zambia (State land and Reserves) Orders, 1928 to 1964*;   99 Year trust Land Rights of occupancy - under *the Zambia (Trust Land) Orders, 1947 to 1964*; and 14 Year leases - under *the Lands and Deeds Registry Act, 1914, Cap. 287.*

Socio - economic relations

Following Ghai (1985), two broad approaches to land can be isolated: one of which sees land as part of the social relations between people and society. This view holds sway in traditional societies which are regulated by customary law and in which subsistence economies predominate.

The second approach views land as a commodity and factor of production. It is found in modern urbanised societies and is regulated by statutory land law. This approach is gaining ground not only in peri-urban areas, but also to a smaller extent, in rural communities.

The development debate has questioned the suitability of customary law in responding to demands of modern development. We will return to this debate under Section 5, below, but first we should highlight some of the major land policy debates.

Discussion of selected major land policy critical debates

Reform of customary tenure

One of the critical questions in land policy relates to the reform of customary land tenure which applies in over 90% of Zambia's total land area of 753,000 sq. Km.

Traditional literature has painted customary tenure as beset with debilitating effect, including that it is uncertain; and it results in unequal distribution of land; that it discourages conservation and improvement of natural resources; that it does not provide security of tenure; that it hinders agricultural development; that it does not encourage the credit and investment necessary in some cases to development; that it perpetuates clan rivalries and tribal divisions; that it acts as a drag on efforts to improve farming methods and that it causes uneconomic fragmentation of land (Mifsud, 1967: 2).

Two fundamentally opposed approaches to reform of customary tenure have been tried out in Africa: individualisation and collectivism. These fall on the extremities of a continuum. Other models may be proposed.

The individualisation model By 'individualisation' is meant the right of an individual to sell, mortgage, lease or otherwise dispose of his land in any manner, in addition to any rights of use he may already enjoy.

The British colonial government supported this model and the East Africa Royal Commission (BARC) 1953-55 helped popularise it. The Commission concluded that:

Policy concerning the tenure and disposition of land should aim
at the individualisation of land ownership, and at a degree of

61

mobility in the transfer and disposition of land which will enable
access to land for its economic use (EARC, 1958: 346)

Following the Commission's Report, a programme of adjudication and
registration of title was rigorously pursued in Kenya. The principles of
private or individual ownership of land were accepted and written into law
and these were viewed as necessary conditions for achieving economic
advance.

As conceived by colonial administrators, individualisation was meant to
create a stable African middle class; to increase security of tenure; to reduce
costs of litigation; to encourage agricultural investment; to enable titles to be
used for credit; to encourage development of a land market; to control land
transfer to ensure an economic size of holding and to control fragmentation
resulting from inheritance (Barrows and Roth, 1989: 6).

However, research evidence has shown that individualisation in Kenya
has not been able to achieve most of the professed objectives. Landlessness
and fragmentation of holdings are still critical (Riddell and Dickerman, 1986:
85); and there has been no firm evidence to support the hypotheses that
individualisation by registration leads to increased investment in agriculture
and to the development of a land market (Barrows and Roth 1989: 19).

In Zambia, there is in existence, in both law and practice, a system for the
individualisation of tenure: there are provisions for obtaining title deeds to
land even in Reserves and Trust Land; but the system is sporadic. Due to the
fact that registration of title is bound to be expensive both in terms of finance
and personnel, it can not be reasonably expected to be implemented
throughout the country at once. An incremental approach is, therefore,
called for.

The collectivisation archetype   This was promoted by Tanzania under
President Nyerere. In 1967, Tanzania adopted a declared official policy of
building a socialist state and embarked on an approach diametrically opposed
to individualisation; generally opting for a collectivist model to rural
development.

This model assumes that an ideal society can be established only through
the transfer of factors of production and powers of decision-making to the
state or other form of community.

It denies private enterprise and negotiability of land. Instead, emphasis is
placed on group motivation and the central planning and control of the

economy and competition, and market forces are assigned no roles in the national economy (Ocram, 1971 & 72: 33; West 1984: 3 and Christodoulou 1990: 66).

Consequent to the socialist policies, Nyerere's government sought to persuade individual peasant farmers to join 'Ujamaa' villages which were intended to develop communal farming; and Nyerere painted a gloomy picture of prospects for individual capitalist farming (Fimbo, 1974: 252).

Claimed advantages of collectivism in Tanzania included that in view of the perception that it was based on social solidarity, it provided a strong force knitting the community together; that it amplified equality of treatment and rejected domination of one man by another; that litigation was kept to a minimum and land speculation was completely excluded; that it solved or avoided the problem of fragmentation and that it allowed the most economic use to be made of capital, mechanisation and management (James and Fimbo, 1973: 93-5).

The critical disadvantage of collectivism may be grounded in Hardin's (1977) 'tragedy of the common's theory'. Although this has been discussed with reference to common pasture, and postulates that it is to be expected that each herdsman will try to keep as many cattle as possible in spite of the resultant overgrazing, it is hereby suggested that its philosophical anchorage extends beyond the use of commons and can cover the general proposition that individuals have less incentive to work hard to produce communal products. In this way, it would seem that collectivism impoverishes nations. It is also capable of reducing people to mere ciphers, by denying them freedom of choice.

Given that the only forms of agricultural organisation that Tanzania was to encourage in endeavours to implement socialism were state and co-operative farms, it necessarily followed that individual ownership of land was officially rejected in favour of common ownership.

However, the economic crisis of the early 1980s, coupled with pressure from the International Monetary Fund (IMF) and other donors, led to a rethinking of land policy, even before the official abandonment of socialism. Thus, in 1983, a new agricultural policy paper introduced a degree of individualism in land ownership and use - the paper set leasehold terms at between 33 and 99 years; Ujamaa villages were to be granted 99 year leases and they were to be given an option to sublet to individuals for terms of 33 to 99 years (Riddell and Dickerman, 1986: 199).

The dismal failure of Ujamaa in Tanzania and Socialism in the former Soviet Union, Eastern Europe and various weakly structured attempts in other African Countries has left the individualisation model epitomised by Kenya as the only viable path of reform for customary tenure. In this sense, West's (1969: 212) argument that "in our present state of knowledge, registration of title is the best we can do to provide stability, security and clarity in land ownership and a basis for the structural and physical planning for the future" seems to have withstood the test of time, so far. Indeed Zambia is following the individualisation path, since it is government policy to encourage people even in rural areas to obtain title deeds.

Nature of statutory interests in land -freehold or leasehold

At independence, Zambia inherited both freehold and leasehold interests; but as seen earlier, under the *Land (Conversion of Titles) Act, 1975, Cap. 289,* freehold tenures were abolished, so that the greatest interests that are now granted by the state are leases for 99 years.

However, the political landscape was altered by the election of the MMD into power in 1991; this professes a new culture in terms of openness of the political system because public debate of important social, economic and political issues now thrives; and the area of land policy has not escaped public scrutiny, as seen earlier.

Questions now current in the area of land policy include whether the existing leasehold system should be continued or whether the country should lean more towards freehold.

To appreciate the arguments which follow, it is important to distinguish freehold from leasehold: a common feature of freehold interests is that they endure for as long as the holder or any of his heirs survive; their duration, therefore, is fixed but uncertain, as one cannot say when they will terminate (Hayton, 1982: 29). In contrast, leaseholds give a right to exclusive possession of land for a fixed or determinable period shorter in duration than the interest of the lessor, that is the person making the grant (Simpson, 1976: 31). The term of years for which exclusive possession is given is normally referred to as a 'lease'.

Historically, the fortunes of time have been dispensing favours between freehold and leasehold, in tune with the political philosophies of governments and the desires and aspirations of the people with respect to bringing about better land tenure and land use.

Thus, before 1928 agricultural land in Northern Rhodesia was alienated to Europeans in freehold. Subsequently, it was granted in both freehold and leasehold, though freehold was restricted to farms along the 'first line of rail' where settlement had already taken place. Small holdings near towns as well as farms off the line of rail were granted on leasehold for periods not exceeding 99 years; but ranches of over 6,000 acres were held for periods of 30 years.

From 1943, the balance tilted in favour of leasehold with the Land Tenure Committee recommending that all future alienations should be for terms of 30 years. But the 1954 Commission of Inquiry into the Future of European Farming Industry recommended the re-introduction of freehold tenure, in respect of agricultural lands. After independence, the UNIP government favoured leasehold tenure and eventually abolished freehold tenures, as indicated above.

In the Third Republic, the old debate between freehold and leasehold has again been rekindled; a call being made for the reintroduction of freehold which condemned existing leasehold system as insecure. This prompted this author' response under the heading "Land is too valuable to give away". The response cautioned against hasty reintroduction of freehold and advised the government to appreciate that land was multidimensional and that some dimensions were not susceptible to business concepts of profit and loss.

Still, both freehold and leasehold offer certain advantages. In respect of freehold, these include that it provides the best form of security for credit; that the sense of absolute ownership it connotes is a powerful incentive to development; that it provides opportunities for large profits to be made when the value of the land has substantially increased; that it confers freedom from control by landlords, whether private or governmental and that it confers status and is sometimes considered as a hall-mark of political freedom, especially where ownership of land (or other property) is an electoral qualification (Meek, 1946: 243-44).

Although critics disparage leasehold tenure for its insecurity and allege that development is consequently inhibited; that loans become difficult to raise; that heirs do not enjoy certainty of undisturbed possession and that it may lead to unfair termination when the lease is in temporary difficulties (Northern Rhodesia, Commission of Inquiry, 1954: 10), proponents argue that land should be regarded as a national asset which it should be the duty of the government to protect, exercising control over its transfer and particularly guarding against its misuse (Northern Rhodesia, Land Tenure

Committee, 1943: 2); that freehold deprives the state of any share of future increments in value (West, 1972: 134)/that man is mortal and has no ethical justification for demanding perpetual interests in land; that leasehold lessens the risk of speculation and underdevelopment; and that while freehold tends to lead to excessive fragmentation, leasehold prevents this through covenants against subletting and subdivision. What is more, under a system of leasehold, the state is able to take steps to meet new conditions and to insist on measures to prevent impoverishment of soil through bad husbandry, overstocking and destruction of forests (Meek, 1946: 244-5).

Zambia - freehold or leasehold? The present government is sending conflicting signals on the preferred type of interest: in 1992, they pledged to continue the leasehold system (Government of the Republic of Zambia, Ministry of Finance, 1992: 17); but the 1994 Budget Speech sent the opposite signal.

On our part, we prefer leasehold to freehold tenure for reasons including that many of the advantages of freehold apply equally well to long leases. This is true of the incentive and profit arguments. Thus, the interests currently granted for 99 years are of such sufficiently long duration that, *ceteris paribus*, a prudent investor would have recouped his investment and profits by the time they lapse. In addition, the main criticism against leasehold tenure, namely, insecurity can be obviated if sufficiently long leases of 99 years continue to be granted on conditions permitting perpetual renewal.

Further, we support leasehold because it is more amenable to programmes of re-planning land use. Such programmes as urban renewal would proceed more smoothly under a system where, at certain times, land reverts to the state which can then re-plan its development.

Conclusion

This paper has highlighted some of the critical questions to be answered in endeavours to formulate land policy. Further, it has attempted to schematically identify the major land policy options in respect of ownership, allocation, use and transfer of land.

On those debates pursued in greater detail, our analysis has led us to support individualisation of tenure by adjudication and registration of title to land rather than collectivism and we have come out in favour of leasehold in preference to freehold.

We must, however, add a rider to our conclusion on the freehold versus leasehold debate; this is that freehold and leasehold tenures are not mutually exclusive; they can co-exist, if it be so decided. In the event that co-existence is preferred, we recommend that grant of freehold be made conditional upon certain minimum standards of development being first achieved. There is precedent for this from the colonial period: *the Agricultural Land Act, 1960, S.26* made provision for leases to be converted to fee simples on fulfilment of certain conditions.

Alternatively, if the two types of interests are allowed to co-exist, a system can be introduced whereby the two interests are separately granted in lands for specific uses. For example freehold can be granted only in respect of residential land while leasehold can be limited to farming or rural land.

Bibliography

Acquaye, E. (1984), 'Principles and Issues.' in Acquaye, E. and Crocombe R. (eds.) *Land Tenure and Rural Productivity in the Pacific Islands*, the University of South Pacific.

Barrows, R. and Roth, M. (1989), 'Land Tenure and Investment in African Agriculture: Theory and Evidence', *Land Tenure Centre*, Paper No, 136.

Christodoulou D. (1990), *The Unpromised Land - Agrarian Reform and Conflict World-wide*, Zed Books Ltd., London.

East Africa Royal Commission, 1953 - 55, (1958), Her Majesty's Stationery Office, Cmd 9475.

Fimbo, G.M. (1974), 'Land, Socialism and Law in Tanzania'. in Ruhumbiaka, G. (ed.), *Towards Ujamaa*, East Africa Literature Bureau, Dar-es-Salaam.

Ghai, Y.P. (1985), 'Land Regimes and Paradigms of Development: Reflections on Melanesian Constitutions', *International Journal of the Sociology of Law*, 13: 393.

Government of the Republic of Zambia (GRZ), Land Commission (1967), *Report of Commission of Inquiry*.

Hardin, G. (1977), 'The Tragedy of the Commons' in Hardin, G. and Baden, J. (eds.) *Managing the Commons*, W.H. Freeman & Co.

Hayton, D.J. (ed.) (1982), *Megarry's Manual of the Law of Real Property*, Stevens & Sons Ltd., London.

James, R.W. and Fimbo, G.M. (1973), *Customary Land Law of Tanzania*, East Africa Literature Bureau, Dar-es-Salaam.

Kaunda, M. (1987), 'Land Tenure Reform in Zambia: Some Theoretical and Practical Considerations', *Cambridge Anthropology*, Vol. 12.

King, R. (1977), *Land Reform: a World Survey*, G. Bell & Sons Ltd, London.

Land Economics Institutes (1960), *Modern land Policy*, University of Illinois Press.

Lichfield, N & Darin-in-Drabkin, H. (1980)., *Land Policy in Planning*, George Allen & Unwin, London.

Meek, C.K. (1946), *Land Law and custom in the Colonies*, University Press, Oxford.

Mifsud, F.M. (1967, 'Customary land law in Africa,' *Food and Agricultural Organisation, Legislative Series*. No. 7. Rome.

Mvunga, P.M. (1980), *The Colonial Foundations of Zambia's Land Tenure System*, Neczam, Lusaka.

Northern Rhodesia Government (NRG), (1943) *Land Tenure Committee Report.*

NRG, Commission of Inquiry (1954), *Report into the Future of the European Farming Industry in Northern Rhodesia on the Issue of Tenure of Agricultural Land.*

Nyerere, J.K. (1969), 'The Arusha Declaration and TANU's Policy on Socialism and Self-reliance' in Svendsen, E.K & Teisen, M. (eds.), *Self-reliant Tanzania*, Tanzania Publishing House, Dar-es-Salaam.

Ocran, T. (1971-2), 'Law, African Development and Social Engineering: a Theoretical Nezus', *Zambia Law Journal*, Vols. 3 & 4.

Ratcliffe, J. (1976), *Land Policy an Exploration of the Nature of Land in Society*, Hutchinson, London.

Riddell, J.C and Dickerman, C. (1986), 'Country Profile of Land Tenure: Africa', *Land Tenure Centre*, paper no. 127.

Simpson, S.R. (1976), *Land Law and Registration*, Cambridge University Press.

West, H.W. (1969), 'The Role of Land Registration in Developing Countries', 102 *Chartered Surveyors.*

West, H. W. (1972), *Land Policy in Buganda.* Cambridge University Press.

6 Housing policy in Zambia

Sylvester M Mashamba

Introduction

The purpose of this paper is to outline the development of the Zambian Housing Policy. In doing so this paper is divided into two main parts: the colonial period and the post-independence era. It must be made very clear from the very beginning, that we also take cognisance of the fact that the study of housing is a very broad-based discipline and any attempt to cover each and every one of its elements in great detail in such a short paper is an impossible feat.

In this connection, therefore, we will only highlight the most important housing policies that were formulated and ignore minor and routine measures. No attempt has also been made to analyse in detail the same policies, but only to make a few observations.

Housing Policy defined

Housing Policy can be defined as a strategy or a plan of action that defines, in specific terms, the goals and means in which housing objectives can be attained.

The qualities of a National Housing Policy (NHP) are best described by A. Van Hoyck when he lists the values as being:

- to achieve a national understanding of the dimensions and implications of Shelter Sector issues among all socio-economic groups concerned by providing a common database and projections for both the public and private sectors;

- to establish a unity of purpose as a basis for decision-making in both the private and public sectors; in this sense, an NHP acts as an agent for co-ordination;
- to establish the place of shelter on the list of national development priorities; shelter has often been left out as a "residue" of other sectors; the formulation of an NHP forces consideration of its right claim on resources and its relationship to other development sectors;
- to define roles and responsibilities of the public and private sector and contribute to the establishment of effective public-private partnerships in the Shelter Sector; and
- to define shelter delivery systems which must serve shelter needs of all income groups throughout human settlements systems; an NHP seeks to eliminate bottlenecks and constraints within the delivery system.

"Efficiency", "Equity" and "Compatibility" rank as the overriding criteria for evaluating shelter and human settlements policies. They guide actions at all decision-making levels.

"Efficiency" connotes the making of steady progress in improving the quality of shelter and human settlement services per unit of resource expenditure.

"Equity" refers to ensuring access to shelter at prices that households can pay without straining their budgets excessively or continuously; shelter allocation policies that satisfy the equity criterion must focus, more especially, on the needs of the lowest income groups in a community.

"Compatibility" requires that shelter and human settlement policies are compatible with others, and that their implementation does not compromise strategies that pursue other major development goals. For example, construction methods that depend on advanced technologies may conflict with policies aimed at stimulating job formation or restricting imports.

Evolution of Housing Policy in Zambia

The Zambian National Housing Policy is a continuum of colonial housing policies and the post-independence perpetuation of similar policies. It is, therefore, imperative that we look at the historical development of housing

71

policies in Zambia if we are to appreciate the prevailing housing situation in Zambia.

It should be understood that urban areas in Zambia are a creation of the colonialists. Some of these colonialists were missionaries like David Livingstone. Livingstone's mission in present day Zambia was to gain support for his personal conception of Christian missionary work in Africa. He was convinced that Africans would be persuaded to accept the Christian faith if their social and economic conditions could be improved to the standard of skills and living styles of Europeans.

Linked to the missionaries work of colonising Africa, was the work of white capitalists, like Rhodes, whose sole interest was to enrich themselves through the extraction of various minerals. It was actually the mining of copper, zinc and lead that attracted more whites to the then Rhodesia. Mining needed African labour, but working for cash was a novelty for Africans and the call for workers did not attract needed labourers. Thus, during the days of labour scarcity, the accepted remedy came to be the "hut tax", which was introduced in 1900 and 1904 in the then North-Western and Northern-Eastern Rhodesias, respectively. The hut tax served the double purpose of encouraging men to work and of contributing to the colonial government's revenues.

The colonialists initially did not bother to provide housing for African workers. They argued that, though wage-earning was necessary for economic growth, Africans should circulate between villages and towns until old age or sickness forced them to retire for good in their rural communities. Workers' wives and families were not allowed to reside in towns. They were expected to remain in rural areas and support themselves from their fields and contributions made by their menfolk in urban areas (Simons, 1976).

The late twenties saw the demand for copper increased, and the world copper prices soar, thus necessitating increased production. This led to the massive creation of more employment opportunities and consequently a corresponding increase in the population of urban Africans in a very short time. These changes presented many problems to the colonial government, especially in the area of housing.

The first documented housing scheme for Africans in the then North-Western Rhodesia was at Malota in Livingstone. It consisted of 476 plots and was laid out in 1916. These were small plots, 15 square metres in area, upon which a number of semi-traditional huts were constructed, frequently occupied by more than one family; communal bucket-type toilets (NHA,

1975). Malota was a typical housing area for Africans working as office orderlies, tea boys, etc., whilst those who worked as house servants were usually housed behind the master's house in servants' quarters. Those employed on farms were housed on the farms.

In 1917, the first Social Welfare Legislation was passed in the then North-Western Rhodesia - the Mines Health and Sanitation Regulations requiring every mine employing more than three hundred (300) Africans to provide adequate accommodation for its workers. African workers compounds were to be kept clean and staffed with a compound manager and a health inspector.

Housing became a privilege for those in regular employment; dismissal or completion of a work contract meant almost certainly instant eviction.

The colonial government further enacted the Municipal Corporation Ordinance (MCO) in 1927 and the Township Ordinance (TO) in 1929. It was hoped that the implementation of these ordinances would make it easier to administer towns and enforce rules dealing with streets, buildings and environmental health, and thus maintain certain "standards" in these towns. The colonial government also enacted a law in 1929: the Employment of Natives Ordinance (ENO) which enforced stricter control of urban African housing, by placing the responsibility of housing workers upon their employers.

It is important to understand here why the colonial government promoted institutional housing which was tied to employment. By placing the responsibility of housing African workers on their employers, the colonial government kept its housing bill to the minimum. Yet it did not place that responsibility on Africans themselves because urban areas were considered to be permanent settlements for whites settlers. But both the employers and local authorities took advantage of the loopholes in these ordinances. Whereas the employers took advantage of the loophole in the ENO which allowed employers to pay their workers a housing allowance in lieu of a company house, local authorities, in turn, took advantage of the establishment of local authority African housing locations under the MCO of 1927 or the TO of 1929, and provided plots of varying sizes and leased them to Africans without restrictions on building materials to be used or the number of dwellings per plot.

Upon realising that the new legislation would encourage more Africans to come to urban areas and settle permanently in these locations, the colonial government passed two new laws which were meant to prevent such a situation from happening: the Native Legislation Ordinance (NLO) of 1929 and the ENO of the same year.

Through the NLO, the colonial government could control the influx of Africans to urban areas by issuing identity certificates which showed whether a native was in employment or not. Those not in employment were sent back to their villages.

Under the ENO of 1929, the colonial government tied housing to employment. The loss of a job normally resulted in instant eviction from a location (Davis: 1933).

In 1933, the colonial government passed the Mine Townships Ordinance (MTO) which declared land that had been occupied by mine companies as separate planning and administrative areas from municipal and township areas. At about the same time, the mining companies realised that African workers could be more productive if they brought their families with them, granted that they could be given suitable accommodation. Here we draw attention to the statement made in 1933 by Sir Auckland Gedders, a copper mining advisor to the Governor, that mining companies wished to stabilise their workforce in the emerging urban society. "Not only could this raise productivity, but it would ensure that the miners lived in better and more humane conditions" (Heisler: 1977). It would also appear that, with the introduction of better machines, it was costing the mines a lot more in terms of lost man-hours and money to be repetitively teaching new groups of African workers to use more sophisticated mining equipment and methods.

However, the Governor's reply was that he was not against "detribalisation" but he was concerned about what would become of the Africans who were unable to return to their native villages if they became unemployed during a slump (Heisler: 1971). From the foregoing, it is evident that while mining companies were trying to stabilise their African labour force for economic reasons, the colonial government's policy was against this development largely for political reasons, or rather to maintain the status quo whereby urban areas were for European settlers, while Africans were considered to be temporary residents.

The first African riots

African grievances against the increased hut tax, low salaries and poor housing for their dependants finally culminated into the first riots in 1935, when miners on the Copperbelt stormed mine compound offices (Parport, 1985).

In the same year (1935) the capital of Northern Rhodesia was transferred from Livingstone to Lusaka. In Lusaka, however, the government seemed to have changed its housing policy for local authority locations, where Africans could build their own houses on local authority land. Africans in Lusaka were actually housed in houses built by the local authority. Two of these locations were Old Kabwata and Old Kamwala built in 1935 and 1937, respectively. Old Kabwata can, therefore, be considered to be the first public housing scheme for urban Africans. All houses in these schemes were single-roomed, circular in shape, and built from sun-dried bricks, with grass roofs and a small kitchen or store attached. Ablution facilities were shared by large numbers of men (Martin: 1974). These houses were meant for bachelors; wives and children were not allowed.

In 1936, the Government implemented its policy of Local Authority Locations (LAL) where African workers were given plots to build their own houses instead of providing them with local authority houses as had happened earlier in Lusaka. In Lusaka 24 plots were made available for African workers in an area called "Mapuloto". Another 1062 plots were made available in Chibuluma, near Kitwe; 220 plots in Fisenge, near Luanshya; 403 plots in Kasompe, near Chingola; 250 plots in Mukobeko, near Kabwe; and 211 plots in Twapia, near Ndola. All these schemes relied on pit latrines and shared water supply, on the basis of one public standpipe for 10-20 houses (N.H.A:1975).

Three (3) years later, the colonial government enacted the Private Location Ordinance (PLO) of 30th June 1939. Under the PLO, an African already established or thereafter established on land in an African housing location could enter into a contract with the landlord, encompassing the right to build a house. The said African was one who was not employed by the land landlord, otherwise the ENO would be more binding.

Within private locations, local authorities had to rely on landlords to control the development of African housing and ensure that those who did so were in genuine employment. This proved difficult to enforce, especially in circumstances where absentee landlords owned these locations. This year may be considered the beginning of uncontrolled settlements, as we shall later see from the recommendations of the Eccles Commission of 1940.

The African strike of 1940

In 1940, African miners went on strike in order to secure better pay, following a similar action by the white miners. Whereas the first five days were relatively peaceful the sixth day was very violent and looting took place.

A commission of inquiry was set up, called the Foster Commission of Inquiry, to investigate the reasons for the strike. The Foster Commission recommended the stabilisation of the urban African population with improved housing for miners' families. It was on the basis of this recommendation that a commission headed by L.W.G. Eccles was subsequently set up to examine the financing and administration of African locations. The commission found that only one tenth of the huts had more than one room. Most fell short of minimum requirements of decency and hygiene, when occupied by married Africans.

The commission's strongest condemnation was made against private locations, and it recommended that they should be subjected to stricter regulation under the provisions of the PLO. The commission further found in some cases, such as in the provision of latrines, that standards fell short of those in South Africa (Tipple, 1981). It recommended higher pay for African workers and economic rents for local authority housing. Other recommendations included the establishment of a link between employment and housing, and the setting up of the Department of African Housing.

Department of Local Government and African Housing

Indeed in 1946, largely as a result of the Eccles Commission's recommendations, a new Department of Local Government and African Housing (DLGAH) was formed. An amount of one million pounds (£1 million) was allocated to this department. The department set up minimum housing standards for accommodating married Africans. Future houses had to consist of two rooms, a combined kitchen and store, a small veranda and a wash house. Each house was to be built on a separate plot of not less than one tenth of an acre, to provide sufficient open space.

These recommendations represented a big step towards the improvement of African housing standards. How was the government going to finance future African housing schemes? It should be noted that this was immediately after the Second World War, when copper prices had once more began to soar. For instance, the price of copper increased from £62 (per ton) in 1946 to £350 in 1955.

Unfortunately for the government, high copper prices resulted in high copper production. Consequently more job opportunities were created for African workers. More Africans thus left their native homes and came to urban areas (more especially to the Copperbelt). This exacerbated African housing problems.

The government, subsequently resorted to building temporary houses, out of which 2,500 were built in 1946 alone. Squalid private locations and unauthorised settlements on private land could not be demolished for the government had no alternative houses and feared to provoke another African riot. It would be wrong if we gave the impression that no "proper" housing was built for Africans during this period. For instance, Old Chilenje in Lusaka was built around this time. It consisted of rectangular grass-thatched houses with two rooms and a veranda. In all 1,533 of such houses were destroyed by heavy rains of that year (Colonial Reports: 1947).

African Migrant Workers Ordinance and the Urban African Housing Ordinance

In 1949, nine thousand permanent brick houses were built out of which 2,500 were for the government's own employees in towns and at district stations, and the other 6,500 were given to local authorities. Those given to local authorities were meant for renting to Africans against loans which had been offered to local authorities at 3.5 percent interest rates, repayable over a forty (40) year period. With a large urban African population (circa. 141,000), 9,000 houses were obviously and extremely inadequate.

Anticipating an influx of more Africans from rural areas, the colonial government passed the African Migrant Workers Ordinance (AMWO) which was intended to control rural-urban African migration levels. The government further reinforced the 1929 ENO by passing the Urban Housing Ordinance (UHO) in 1948. The UHO obliged every person employing married Africans to provide suitable quarters at his own expense. At the same time it obliged every local authority to establish one or more African housing areas for the accommodation of Africans employed within their boundaries. Employers were further required to provide water and sanitary services on a non-profit making basis to all African housing within their areas. Communal toilets were not permitted in any African housing area, save in housing areas reserved for single persons or in hostels.

The government was at this time trying to seal existing loopholes that had been created in the PLO of 1929 by placing African housing areas under local authority control. Responsibilities placed under the local authorities included, among other things, administration and maintenance of minimum standards in those areas. The central government was essentially relieving itself of the burden of housing the thousands of urban Africans.

Meanwhile, the government, through the newly created African Housing Department, continued to provide formal houses for Africans in urban areas. In Lusaka, New Chilenje (1950-53); Chimwemwe (1955-70), Kamitondo (1950-55), and Kwacha (1955-59) in Kitwe, were some of the housing areas built for the African labour force. All these housing schemes were built according to the 1948 Urban African Housing Ordinance. Houses consisted of one or two bedrooms, with a small kitchen, a veranda and a pit latrine.

In 1956, the government established the Northern Rhodesia African Housing Board (NRAHB), the forerunner to the National Housing Authority (NHA) with the responsibility of design and erection of housing for Africans in the then Northern Rhodesia in collaboration with, or on behalf of local authorities. While appreciating this generous gesture to African housing policy by the colonial government, it is important not to lose sight of the serious repercussions that this had on informal housing development. As better and more expensive houses were built for Africans, it meant that fewer houses could be built overall. Yet the urban population was increasing rapidly. Further, the construction boom of the 1950s also meant a corresponding increase in employment opportunities for Africans.

For instance, most informal settlements that sprung up during the fifties (50s) were started as building contractors compounds. Van Huizen, Brickfields (1950), Ichimpe Plantation (1957), Brickfield (Garneton),

Zambia Clay, Mackenzie, Charlie West (1952) and the Old Water Works (1940) are examples of contractors compounds that eventually became the nucleus for the rapid growth of informal settlements.

The construction of more formal housing for Africans in urban areas also resulted in the creation of more squatter settlements for charcoal vendors. Soon, therefore, there was a big market for charcoal and those migrants who failed to find formal employment turned to charcoal burning. Considering that most charcoal-burners settlements were located outside local authority boundaries, local authorities turned a blind eye to their presence. In Kitwe for example, Mufuchani, Mutupa. Chamwanza, Dennis, Kamatipa and Sawyers were settlements which began charcoal burning areas.

The mushrooming of informal settlements in the mid fifties can also be attributed to government's policy of reducing housing subsidies in 1955 and 1956, and their complete withdrawal in 1958. It was hoped that this move would encourage more Africans to build their own houses (Colonial Reports: 1958). But this was wishful thinking as it should be remembered that most urban dwellers were migrants in search of jobs and without money. It was also a fallacy to expect Africans to build solid structures in urban areas when they were regarded as temporary residents.

The copper mines, the biggest employers of Africans were also concerned with the cost involved in providing housing to every African employee. Sir Ronald Prain, Chairman of the then Rhodesia Selection Trust in 1956 is quoted to have said, "The capital outlay required from employers in order to house a rapidly growing African population is frightening, it may tend to make Copperbelt mines high cost producers with the attendant consequences of African housing actually inhibiting the development of secondary industries". He thought that the development of home-ownership schemes for Africans would be more satisfactory, but he did not explain how they could afford these houses under the proposed scheme at their low wages (Simons, 1976).

In 1963, a year before Independence, the first African census was conducted which revealed that there were approximately 3,405,800 Africans in Northern Rhodesia and that 20.5% lived in urban areas.

Post-independence housing policies

At independence, travel restrictions on Africans were removed through Article 24 of the new constitution which stated that "No person shall be deprived of his freedom of movement". The net result was that there was a massive increase in the urban population due to migration from rural areas. Between 1963-1969 the percentage of urban population increased from 20.5 percent to 29 percent. During the same period, the annual growth rate of urban population reached 8.9 percent whilst that of the rural population was only 0.5 percent

While urban population was increasing in thousands of people per year, the best that urban local authorities could achieve in building houses was only 5,100 to 6,000 low cost houses per year (Robertson, 1978) so that most migrants in the urban areas were left with no choice but to build their own houses in informal settlements, commonly referred to as squatter areas. In Lusaka for example, the proportion of the population living in informal settlements increased from 16 percent in 1963, to 35 percent in 1970, and to about 42 in 1972.

In 1970, the Deputy Town Clerk of Lusaka openly acknowledged the inadequacy of the supply of public housing, noting that the council's housing waiting list had increased since 1965 from 8,000 to 21,000 families; he went further to describe the housing shortage as "desperate and pathetic" (Seymour: 1976). In 1972, the waiting list for council housing was 22,000 and the informal housing population was 60,000 (Gertzel, Baylies and Szeftel: 1984).

It was against this background that the post independence Zambian Government formulated its first housing policy. The first housing policy in Zambia was contained in the Transitional Development Plan (TDP) for the period commencing January 1965 to June 1966, a period of 18 months. Under the TDP period, Government committed £8.1m from a total budget of £45.9m to housing which represented 17.65% of the national budget. Under this policy plan, government envisaged spending £3.5m on urban housing with some of this money going towards new housing and some on improvements to existing ones.

Nearly 5,000 new houses were to be built in the towns lying along the line of rail, with just over half the total planned for the Copperbelt , one quarter for Lusaka. The government also set aside money for lending to urban local authorities for house building. These loans were meant for urban authorities that could meet the interest and repayment charges. A further one million pounds (£1 million) was set aside for Civil Servants to either build or buy houses. The practice of tying housing to employment was once more being extended from the colonial days.

The other thrust of this policy was aimed at the elimination of all informal settlements and the raising of building standards. Unfortunately for the new government, in 1965 Ian Smith unilaterally declared independence for Southern Rhodesia, Zambia joined the rest of the world in imposing sanctions on Rhodesia. Zambia depended on Rhodesia and South Africa for its major imports and export routes for copper.

Furthermore, in 1968 and 1969 the post independence government formulated the Mulungulushi and Matero Reforms, respectively. Amongst the other things, expatriate enterprises were denied credit facilities and renewal of their licences was dependent upon the production of evidence that there were Zambian shareholders in these companies. In the construction industry, the government decided that all building contracts worth less than £50,000 could only be given to Zambians.

Major building companies were also bought out by the government through the purchase of at least 51 percent of the shares. Other companies that dealt with building materials were nationalised and amalgamated into a state company called: Zambia Steel and Building Supplies Ltd. The government further amended the law to empower it to acquire property compulsorily subject to the payment of compensation and, to pay no such compensation in respect of undeveloped land or land belonging to absentee landlords.

Many companies were nationalised and as a result, many expatriate and white residents lost faith in the government and left the country. But with less than 0.5 percent of the 3.5 million African population who had attained a full primary education standard, a mere 961 with Cambridge School Certificates, and less than 100 university graduates, the country embarked on a premature Zambianisation programme. The net result was a low level of capital formation rate in the economy which also affected housing.

The above events led the government in 1965 to enact its first informal housing policy, after realising that they could not satisfy urban housing needs with formal housing. The Government, therefore, produced Circular 17 of 1965, which stated that 30 percent of the 6,000 housing plots to be provided per year in the next five years were to be sites and services plots i.e. 1,800 plots. Local authorities were to receive 50 percent subsidies for servicing plots from the government.

Continued urban growth through rural-urban migration and the failure of government housing delivery systems led to the issuing of Circular 59 of 1966 which called for the construction of up to 20,000 self-help houses in 1967 and each subsequent year, thereafter. Local authorities were required to ensure that the bulk of their high density houses were to be built through self help.

The first national development plan, 1966-1970

The effects of sanctions on Rhodesia and the termination of trade agreements with the "White South" were already being felt. For instance, the average cost of a high density institutional house had risen from £320 in 1965 to £800 in 1966 (G.R.Z/FNDP: 1966-1970). The unsatisfied housing need in urban areas was then running at 46,000. These grim statistics led to the government's policy of advocating the development of more "normal" sites and services schemes. The government actually went further to propose and effect the lowering of plot service standards in these schemes. The objective was to effect economies so as to enable a greater number of plots to be made available from the limited funds available.

The government further made available £1.3 million for loans to people settling on sites and services schemes to assist them to complete the building of their homes in more permanent materials. This loan was, however, open only to those settling on urban schemes. In the meantime, the population in informal settlements was growing at 30 percent annually. Hence in 1968 the government produced Circular 294 of 1968: "Resettlement of Squatters" which clearly stated the government's intention to resettle all squatters in "basic" sites and services areas.

During this period, high standard institutional and formal houses were also put up, for instance, Libala and Chilenje South in Lusaka.

The second national development plan, 1972-1976

The most notable policy measure under the Second National Development Plan (SNDP) was the recognition by government that "although squatter areas were unplanned they nevertheless represented assets both in social and financial terms" (GRZ/SNDP: 1972-76). Nevertheless, the government did state in the SNDP that squatter settlements now required re-planning and the provision of services, and that the wholesale demolition of good and bad houses alike was not a practical solution. The plan's first priority was the acquisition of land, whenever any informal settlement was to be upgraded.

Strict control of further settlement growth was to be enforced both inside and outside the designated areas. The following services were meant for all upgraded squatter settlements: piped water, water-borne sewerage and sewage disposal systems, roads and surface water drainage, street lighting and other communal services. Above all, this policy assured illegal settlers security of tenure to land. In all about 25,000 households benefited from this strategy.

Housing (Statutory and Improvement Areas) Act of 1974

In 1974, the government enacted the Housing (Statutory and Improvement Areas) Act (HSIAA) which assured households in sites and services schemes and in upgraded areas legal title to the land on which they had built their houses.

The HSIAA stated that the Minister (of Local Government and Housing) may by statutory order declare any area of land within the jurisdiction of a Council to be a statutory housing area and that he may at any time, therefore, declare that the whole or part of the land comprised in affected housing areas, to be part of the Statutory Housing Area. In the same manner, the Minister was further empowered by the Act to declare any area an improvement area or otherwise. There are two prerequisites to this act. Firstly, that the area must be leased from the state, and secondly, that the local authority responsible must prepare a statutory housing area plan or improvement area plan, as the case may be.

Occupiers of land in statutory housing areas were granted a 99 year lease, whereas those in improvement areas were granted 30 years. Unfortunately the 30 years leases are not recognised by the Zambia National Building Society for purposes of getting housing loans.

Successes and failures of the upgrading scheme

Other notable features of the informal housing policy implementation were that physical improvements were made to thousands of houses because of the infrastructure services that were provided. Unfortunately the most striking failures of the scheme were manifest in the cost recovery exercise. It should be mentioned here that the One-Party State political machinery played a vital role in frustrating the cost recovery exercise. For instance, UNIP leaders campaigned against the enforcement of monthly loan repayments thorough evictions. Local (party) leaders at the section level also campaigned and mobilised people against settling service-charge increases. Party leaders obviously found political advantage in campaigning and mobilising people against Council policies as this won them more votes from residents. By 1980 only 125 families out of 7,400 had cleared all their arrears and became eligible for land occupancy licences.

The third and fourth national development plans

The Third National Development (TNDP) covered the period 1979-1983 and the Fourth National Development Plan (FONDP) was between 1989-1993. In essence, the two policy plans did not produce any new housing measures except to recycle the same old ideas which were:

- The attainment of at least minimum Shelter Standards;
- The promotion of low-income group housing;
- The promotion of home-ownership schemes financed from personal savings;
- The promotion of rural housing as an integral part of the rural development strategy;
- The promotion of institutional housing;
- The establishment of a housing bank for assisting low-income earners.

While the above policy measures were well intended, their actual implementation was pathetic to say the least. No institutional framework was set up to follow through and implement the policy. In many cases what was done on the ground was totally different from what was proposed. For instance, whilst K50 million was allocated for infrastructure and communal services for site and service schemes, only 25 million was actually spent; similarly, whereas an amount of K5m was allocated for squatter upgrading, yet only K1.6m was spent. But when it came to institutional housing the allocated sum was K100m but the actual expenditure exceeded K140 million.

In some cases, policy measures tended to contradict each other. For example, one strategy advocated for the construction of more institutional housing while another advocated for the more home-ownership schemes within the same policy statement.

In other words, these policies were rather too ambitious because they did not accord well with the resources at the government's disposal, as indicated in the table below.

It should also be noted that although Zambia pioneered in squatter upgrading schemes in Africa in the middle 1970s, the government continued to pursue the policy of demolishing informal housing through various squatter control units in each local council, thus rendering the implementation the HSIAA of 1974 irrelevant.

Implementation of the TNDP and FNDP housing programmes

HOUSING TYPE	TARGETS	ACHIEVEMENT	SHORTFALL	% ACHIEVED
A. Serviced Plots	14,600	4,963	9,63734.0	34.0
B. Upgraded Units (Squatters)	110,900	13,1629	7,73911.9	11.9
C. Low Income Units	26,700	3,500	23,200	13.1
D. Other Lower, Middle Income Units	7,000	700	6,300	10.0
E. Very Low Units	250,300	0	250,300	0.0

Source: Ministry of Decentralisation and Housing and National Housing Authority.

The MMD and its housing policy

The MMD government, ever since assuming power in 1991, did not formulate any housing policy until January, 1996. Until then, the government had pursued the enabling shelter development strategy, which strategy or policy advocated the removal of direct Government involvement in the actual construction of shelter. Instead the government's interest had to be concentrated on formulating policy measures for facilitating the provision of adequate shelter for all (see also the next chapter).

But even an enabling shelter development policy requires that certain roles are played by government and that access to housing by vulnerable groups is assured. Instead, the government's enabling shelter development strategy means leaving the provision of housing in the hands of speculative developers. The government has even gone to the extent of repealing those sections of the Employment Act which previously compelled employers to provide tied housing to their employees.

Conclusion

It has already been mentioned that, in the main, housing policies that have been pursued since Zambia's attainment of independence have been customised to the Zambian environment, at least on paper. It is, therefore, proposed to reinforce them by including the following suggestions into future national housing policies:

- The promotion of the use of indigenous building materials and the adoption of updated and realistic building standards.
- The mobilisation of public and private finance for use in the housing market.
- The encouragement of small-scale businessmen and private enterprise to participate in the housing delivery mechanism.
- The formulation and adoption of affordable and sustainable housing policies.
- The introduction of market-led forces into the housing sector but with the mandate that the government be obliged to intervene in the provision of housing to the lowest income and vulnerable groups.

- The incorporation of the informal housing sector as an integral part of the overall national housing policy.

The myth in the traditional Zambian housing policy has been: that by formulating and adopting high standards for shelter construction, informal housing and settlements, which are considered to represent advanced signs of environmental blight and political failures, will be eradicated. The implementation of this dream could make sense if adequate shelter, infrastructure and human settlements standards were affordable and sustainable. Past Zambian experience has demonstrated that the use of present building and planning standards which were inherited from colonial days is irrelevant and inadequate for solving contemporary housing and human settlements problems.

The traditional Zambian policy has also failed to provide adequate shelter at prices that the poor can afford. The only viable way in which vulnerable households can be adequately sheltered in Zambia is through incremental house construction by the urban poor themselves, as demonstrated by some of the people-centred initiatives in shelter and infrastructure development in Part 2 of the next chapter.

Bibliography

Davies, M J (1933), *Modern Industry and the African*, Frank Carr and Co. Ltd., London.

Gertzel, C, C Baylies and M Szeflel, (1984), *The Dynamics of the One Party State in Zambia*, Manchester University Press, Manchester.

Heisler, H, (1977), 'The Creation of a Stabilised Urban Society: A turning point in the Development of Northern Rhodesia/Zambia', *African Affairs* 70 (279) pp. 124-145.

Hobbs, F D, and J F Doling (1981), *Planning for Engineers and Surveyors*, Pergamon Press.

Martin, R, (1974), *Local Government in Zambia*, Lusaka City Council, Lusaka, pp. 53 - 94.

National Housing Authority, (1975), *Urban Sanitation Survey*, National Housing Authority, Lusaka.

Parport, J L, (1986), 'The Household and the Mine Shaft: Gender and Class Struggle on the Zambian Copperbelt, 1926-64', in, *Journal of Southern African Studies*, Vol. 13 No.1 pp. 36-56, Oct. 1986.

Seymour, T, (1976), 'The Causes of Squatter Settlements: The case of Lusaka, Zambia in an International Context', in *Slums or Self Reliance? Urban growth in Zambia, Communication No. 12* pp. 1-26, University of Zambia, Institute for African Studies, Lusaka.

Simons, H J , (1976), 'Zambia's Urban Situation', in *Slums or Self-reliance? Urban Growth in Zambia, Communication No. 12* pp. 1-26, University of Zambia, Institute for African Studies, Lusaka.

Simons, H J, (1979), 'Zambia's Urban Situation', in Development in Zambia, pp. 1-24, Turok B. Ed. Zed Press, London .

Tipple, A G, (1981), 'Colonial Housing Policy and the "African Towns" of the Copperbelt, the Beginnings of Self-Help', in *African Urban Studies* 11 (fall) pp. 354 - 36.

Tipple, A G, (1977), 'Mufuchani - A Squatter Settlement in Zambia' *Habitat International*, Vol. 2 No. 586 pp. 543-546, Pergamon Press, Great Britain.

Willis, A J, (1985), *An introduction to the History of Central Africa: Zambia, Malawi and Zimbabwe*, University Press, Oxford.

Zambia, Republic of, (1989), *Fourth National Development Plan 1989 - 1993*, Government Printer, Lusaka.

Zambia, Republic of, (1965), *Transitional Development Plan* (Jan. 1965-June 1966) Government Printer, Lusaka.

Zambia, Republic of, (1971), *Second National Development Plan* (Jan. 1965 - June 1966), Government Printer, Lusaka.

Zambia Republic of, (1966), *First National Development Plan* (1966 - 1970), Government Printer, Lusaka, 1966.

Zambia, Republic of, (1965), 'High Density Housing Areas - Site and Service Schemes', *Ministry of Mines* , Circular Ref. CD 1536/17, October, 1965.

7   Towards a sustainable urbanisation policy for Zambia

C Pule Katele

PART ONE : "SUSTAINABLE DEVELOPMENT" CONCEPTS

Introduction

There has been no clearly defined urbanisation policy in Zambia over the past ninety years. Consequently, highly unsustainable urbanisation patterns have evolved, especially, over the past two decades. This paper, therefore, sets out to examine the concept of "sustainable development" as a basis for formulating, adopting and implementing a sustainable urbanisation policy for Zambia. The implementation of such a policy should enable the country to develop on a stable political basis and prosper economically into the Twenty First Century.

As with the review of the "National Housing Policy" paper, it would be nigh impossible to address all issues of urbanisation in this short paper. However, basic steps such as policies and strategies for land, shelter, infrastructure, poverty reduction, social equity, and democratic governance being essential ingredients for the successful formulation of a sustainable urbanisation policy, are briefly discussed in this paper.

Part 1 of this paper introduces the concept of "sustainable development" and its extension to the development of human settlements.

An assessment of existing human settlements conditions over the past two decades (1975-1995) and of on-going initiatives in the "sustainable development" of human settlements in Zambia is made above.

Counterpart policies and strategies for the formulation of a national urbanisation policy for ushering the country's development processes into the Twenty First Century are discussed in Part 2 of this paper.

Part 2 of this paper is based on the "National Report" on shelter and human settlements conditions in Zambia which was edited on behalf of the Zambian Government by the author. The report was presented to the Habitat II Conference which was organised by the United Nations Centre for Human Settlements (UNCHS-Habitat) from 3rd to 14th June, 1996 in Istanbul, Turkey.

Issues of major concern

Although urban areas in Zambia, especially mining towns, have served as prime sources of economic growth, this growth has, however, taken place without serious regard to negative social and environmental problems which have been generated in the process of achieving economic growth, more especially, through recent urbanisation patterns.

It is estimated that Zambia's urban population has risen from zero per cent at the turn of the century, to 20.5 per cent in 1963, and to 42 per cent by 1990. The proportion of Zambia's population which may live in urban areas will exceed 50 per cent by the year 2,000.

Enormous population increases which have taken place since the 1960s have been characterised not only by environmental degradation, but also by deepening levels of poverty, social inequality, the deteriorating quality of shelter, public services and social amenities in towns, cities and the country as a whole.

The difficulties posed by rapid urbanisation trends lie in finding short term solutions for enhancing economic growth while solving the problems of poverty, social inequality and environmental degradation which continue to haunt human settlements in Zambia.

Definitions of "sustainable development"

Evolution of "sustainable development" concepts

The concept of "sustainable development" has evolved from principles of environmental conservation. Environmental conservation principles have evolved from time immemorial. The "sustainable development" concept is an issue which has permeated the vocabulary of almost all professions; and moreover, it is a concept which is subjected to impassioned rhetoric and has, subsequently, had its meaning seriously distorted.

The concept gradually came to assume great importance in the work ethics of development planners from the following publications:

- "The limits of growth" by the Massachusetts Institute of Technology in 1973,
- "Blue Print for Survival" by "Ecologist" a British magazine in 1973;
- "Only one earth" by Dame Barbara Ward in 1972;
- "Small is Beautiful" by Ernest Schumacher in 1973,
- The UN Conference on Habitat in Vancouver in 1976, and
- The UN Conference on Desertification in 1977 (Welbank: 1994: 13).

The concept finally emerged after the completion of the report by the International Union for the Conservation of Nature (IUCN) in 1980. The IUCN report marked a turning point in the work ethics of development planners from the classic economic approach which had hitherto advocated the philosophy of maximum exploitation of natural resources in order to achieve economic growth. The market-led economy lobby group is extremely powerful in Zambia, especially under the current Government's economic policy. In other words, economic growth has to be attained without regard to the intolerable negative social and environmental impacts that this growth would generate, or the environmental costs that would be passed on to future generations.

Instead, the IUCN's report was re-oriented towards the sustainable management of the natural environment and the mitigation or reversal of human impacts upon it. The report concluded that "people could use natural resources such as species and ecosystems, at levels and ways which would allow them to renew themselves indefinitely" (IUCN-UNEP-WWF:1980).

Subsequently, the UN General Assembly created the World Commission on Environmental Development (WCED) in 1983 . The WCED set out to explore relationships which had hitherto emerged between the vigorous pursuit of economic growth, measured in terms of indicators such as per capita income, household expenditure, etc., and their impacts on the environment. As a result of these initiatives, the WCED emerged with a new definition of "sustainable development" which was: " Development that meets the needs of the present without compromising the ability of future generations to meet their own needs" (WCED, 1987:43).

The consolidation of new concepts on "sustainable development" happened at the United Nations Commission for Environmental Development's (UNCED) conference held in May 1992 at Rio de Janeiro. A range of environmentally-friendly agreements were concluded, the most important of which was the Local Agenda 21. Agenda 21, as it would become popularly known, was an action plan which set out guidelines of what countries should do in order to achieve "sustainable development" in the Twenty First Century (UNCED, 1992: Chapter 7)

The principles of Agenda 21, among others, recognise that "the overall human settlement objective is to improve the social, economic and environmental quality of human settlements and the living and working environment for people (UNCED, 1992: para 7.4).

Criteria for evaluating "sustainable development"

Attainable criteria for the "sustainable development" of human settlements may, among others, therefore, include:
- the adoption of low-impact lifestyles and technologies;
- making continuous availability of land for development;
- the use of environmentally sound infrastructure, and waste management systems;
- making increasing efficient use of energy through recycling and renewable sources;
- a culture of safety with respect to disasters; and
- the enhancement of human potential through training and empowerment (UNCHS/15/6:1995:4).

Hardoy and others (UNCHS/15/6:1995:4) argued further that, if the concept of sustainable human settlements is to be more meaningful, it must be redefined to include elements of basic human needs .These include:

- freedom of choice and participation in local and national decision-making to ensure access by urban residents to adequate shelter, a healthy environment, and basic services; and

- access to employment opportunities, all within a framework of human dignity and human rights (UNCHS/C/15/6:1995:4).

The Brundtland Commission (WCED:1987) took the argument further by emphasising that highest priority be given to the poor: by raising their standard of living - especially the standard of living of the least advantaged in society.

Three cornerstones for the sustainable development of human settlements

From the foregoing arguments it would appear that consensus among planners has finally been reached on the principal criteria for the "sustainable development" of human settlements. The "sustainable development" of human settlements appears to depend on three cornerstones, namely: social, economic and environmental sustainability.

Considerable reporting on the environmental sustainability of human settlements has taken place, while less debate has arisen on the economic and social sustainability of human settlements, despite significant places that these issues occupy in the development of human settlements.

Socially sustainable human settlements

With regard to the social sustainability of human settlements, it has been argued that an absence of 'peace' in the development of human settlements may render them unsustainable. In other words, the presence of economic and social injustice, social segregation and inequality may lead to social tension and unrest, political instability and other man-made disasters. Angola, Burundi, Liberia, Somalia, Sudan and Rwanda, to name a few countries, are clear examples of African states where socially unsustainable lifestyles in the development of human settlements are taking place due to an absence of 'peace'.

In short, the presence of 'peace', characterised by democratic governance, accountability and transparency are the necessary ingredients for the development of socially sustainable human settlements.

Economically sustainable human settlements

Housing development uses the largest proportion of land (usually between 60 and 80 per cent in Zambian towns) in the development of human settlements once it is realised that housing includes: land, shelter, and community infrastructure. It is, therefore, logical to use key housing indicators as the basis for assessing the quality of human settlements.Indicators for the economic sustainability of housing development include: affordability, accessibility and replicability.

Accessibility, in housing terms, means that target households for a housing project would gain full access to adequate shelter after the project has been implemented.

Affordability, again in housing terms, means that the cost of providing housing would be reduced to a level where the target households would be able and willing to pay for shelter, without straining their budgets and other resources.

Replicability, in housing terms again, means that target households would be able and willing to pay for housing with minimum or no outside financial and technical help.

It follows, therefore, that an economically unsustainable housing project is the type which may not be successfully developed, operated and maintained on local resources, and would collapse if external funding and technical support, for instance, were withdrawn (UNCHS/15/6:1995:7).

Environmentally sustainable human settlements

Criteria for evaluating environmentally sustainable human settlements are wide and varied, and generally include those indicated in paragraph 1.3.2. In addition, consideration must be given to the choice of infrastructure and the use of technology which is compatible with environmental sustainability criteria, as follows:

- Technology which uses renewable resources is more preferable to that which relies on non-renewable resources.

- Technology which is simple and appropriate to users is more preferable to complex and high technology.
- Technology which relies on the use of cleaner and environmentally friendly resources is more preferable to that which has dirty impacts.
- Technology which depends on external financial and technical support, especially hard currencies, expatriate labour and imported materials, is less preferable to the use of lacal resources.
(UNCHS/15/6: 1995: 6).

Relevance of sustainable development concepts to human settlements in Zambia

Although Zambian cities and towns consume a disproportionate amount of natural resources, and are at the same time major sources of activities which degrade the natural environment, they are nevertheless the main generators of economic growth, once it is realised that urban-based economic activities have consistently contributed between 50 and 80 per cent to the Gross Domestic Product (GDP) of Zambia between 1985 and 1991 (National Accounts Statistical Bulletin No.3 of 1990 and No. 4 of 1992. Both the built and natural environments represent economic resources for the present and future generations. In view of the superior advantages that built environments such as cities and towns have over rural areas, they will continue to attract rural migrants in large numbers (GRZ:CSO:NASB:1990 and 1992).

Some migrants will find suitable employment in the formal sector of the economy. However, the majority will end up in the informal economic and social sectors, and face limited access to adequate housing in informal settlements. These settlements are usually located on land which may not be environmentally suitable. Socio-economic lifestyles that are found in informal settlements are unacceptable as they fall short of the principal criteria for the sustainable development of human settlements.

Conclusion

From the foregoing discussion, it should be evident that to formulate a sustainable urbanisation policy requires not only the inclusion of social and economic development objectives which must be achieved in the short term period, but also long term strategies for the sustainable development of human settlements. In other words, the sustainable development of human settlements requires that: short term market-led economic gains should be carefully balanced against long term benefits for this and future generations.

PART TWO: TOWARDS A SUSTAINABLE URBANISATION POLICY

Introduction

The Government has very limited resources to meet all the needs of the Zambian people. It must, therefore, select a limited number of priority areas where available scarce resources must be invested in order to facilitate the sustainable development of human settlements.

The broad goal

The Government's overall goal must be to improve living conditions for all people in Zambia on a sustainable basis.

The main objective

The Government's main objective must be to facilitate the sustainable development of human settlements in Zambia. To achieve this objective requires a radical shift from the culture of dependency on the State towards community participation in the socio-economic development of human settlements. People should be empowered further to shoulder the responsibilities of improving their own living conditions.

Specific objectives

To achieve the above objective, the following targets should be attained.

Governance   The pillars of democratic governance - transparency, accountability and efficiency - must be strengthened under the constitutional, public service and socio-economic reform programs, and through supporting administrative, institutional and legal reforms. Improved   governance will result in political stability and economic prosperity.

Intensified civic education   An intensified nation-wide civic education campaign, through the organisation of at least two seminars (and similar activities) each year at provincial, district and community levels, must be mounted to sensitise people on the merits of implementing community-based development programs. A successful civic education campaign would enhance the spirit of self-reliance in the mobilisation of dormant resources for development.

Promotion of labour-intensive economic activities   The Government must encourage the development of small-scale agricultural and labour-intensive industries such as those being promoted through the Agricultural Sector Investment Program (ASIP), Small Industry Development Organisation (SIDO) and Village Industries Service (VIS), and provide a more conducive environment for the development of other private and informal economic activities, until the GNP per capita exceeds the UN's global poverty datum line of US $600 per annum. The successful promotion of these activities would generate more employment opportunities and greater economic prosperity in the country.

Improved public infrastructure   Priority must be placed by the Government on the achievement of the following minimum investment targets in the development of:

- housing (from 0.3 per cent in 1987 to over 6 per cent of the GDP by the year 2000),
- water and sanitation (from 76 per cent in 1993 to over 90 per cent access level in urban areas by the year 2000);
- transport and communications (from 3.8 per cent in 1980-85 to over 10 per cent of the GDP by the year 2000);
- energy (from 3.1 per cent in 1980-85 up to over 5 per cent of the GDP by the year 2000) .

Dependable social safety-nets Reliable and easily accessible social safety-nets must be established to assist households that may be facing transitional and structural poverty. The broadening of dependable social safety-nets such as The Programme Against Malnutrition (PAM), Programme Urban Self-Help (PUSH), etc., would enable households that are temporarily or permanently unable to fend for themselves, prior to their rehabilitation, to be integrated in their communities. The support of the International Community, Non-Governmental Organisations (NGOs) and Community-Based Organisations (CBOs) during the implementation of the Government's community participation programs will continue to play an important part in serving marginalised and vulnerable groups.

Efficient planning systems Socio-economic and environmental planning systems must be upgraded, and a realistic balance struck between the pursuit of short term market-led economic benefits against long-term sustainable development processes. The establishment of efficient resource planning, implementation and management systems at provincial, district and community levels will lead to the sustainable development of human settlements.

Conclusion

The adoption and implementation of the community participation strategy is a giant step for moving away from the culture of dependency on the State towards finding solutions for raising institutional capacities, and the reduction of fundamental causes of poverty. People-centered initiatives should be given highest priority in order to alleviate poverty and attain the sustained development of human settlements in Zambia.

Counterpart strategies and policies

Government involvement

The Government, through its local authorities, with the involvement of NGOs, CBOs and other stakeholders, must play a leading part in facilitating the development of sustainable human settlements. These institutions need adequate funding, effective planning and organisation in order to exist and deliver their services efficiently.

Capacity building

There is an urgent need to enhance the capacity of communities at all levels of human settlements to effectively participate in the socio-economic development of their areas. People must be empowered to make decisions that affect their living conditions, be enabled to mobilise affordable resources for the development of shelter, and for the provision, operation and maintenance of community infrastructure.

Capacity building is also urgently needed to strengthen local administration, governance and management.

Appropriate legal and institutional frameworks

The Government must adopt and implement appropriate legal frameworks within which the development of sustainable human settlements should take place. This step could be achieved through the Government's commitment to the establishment of adequate and effective institutional frameworks at all levels of governance.

In short, the Government must empower local communities, particularly the less privileged, to make decisions that affect their local development, and the provision of community infrastructure. It must, therefore, legislate for necessary institutional and legal frameworks to support community participation in the development and provision of community infrastructure.

Poverty reduction initiatives and the generation of economic growth

Within the context of poverty reduction, the provision of services which promote economic development would be an important task if the types of services to be provided, organisations to be involved, and specified standards of service delivery were clearly defined. The Government must ensure that appropriate mechanisms for service delivery are clearly defined so that vulnerable groups will be enabled to take an active part in the definition, delivery and maintenance of services to be provided.

In rural areas, the Government must facilitate the provision of services such as credit, extension and marketing through ASIP and the stakeholders. Improved access to these services will enable the rural population to become more productive in the current liberalised market economy. The implementation of this strategy will not only help to curb rural-urban migration, but also lower rural poverty conditions.

In urban areas, the initiation of own economic development activities must be facilitated through NGOs, CBOs and the stakeholders, especially at the household level. The provision of services like transport, energy, and water will make a positive impact on the vulnerable groups who will then be enabled to initiate their own economic development activities.

The adoption and implementation of these strategies will help to reduce poverty levels for the majority of the low-income households. Improved income generation opportunities that are provided in the current liberalised economic system should facilitate easy access by the vulnerable groups to community facilities such as water, education, health and other social services which have to be paid for.

Social development

The provision of a variety of adequate social amenities form a vital part of any prosperous human settlement. These amenities are the life-blood of any given settlement which must sustain its growth. These amenities must include: hospitals and schools, shops, spiritual development, recreational and entertainment centres, and various civic and cultural facilities. An adequate provision of social facilities will in turn lead to the generation of more investment and employment opportunities, and the sustainable development of human settlements.

Land and housing delivery policies

The Government must facilitate improved access to land, security of tenure (including that of established squatters in environmentally acceptable settlements), and affordable adequate shelter for the majority of the Zambian people. Existing informal land trading procedures must be recognised, and thus legalise land trading, and reduce high rent-seeking speculative development.

Clearly defined land user rights for specified periods are important and must be put in place to ensure equitable land distribution patterns. More land must be released and serviced for housing purposes, and the highest priority in allocation procedures must be accorded to women and vulnerable households.

Building regulations must be reviewed to accord well with affordable building standards, the use of labour-intensive technologies, and local building materials in the housing construction industry.

Environmental infrastructure development policy

There is an opportunity in Zambia to complement Government efforts in providing safe drinking water and improved sanitation methods by building on the technical knowledge of NGOs which are already working in low-income settlements.

The Government must decentralise, privatise, where feasible, and facilitate the provision of safe drinking water to more households. Priority should be accorded to the provision of potable water to low-income housing areas as it is essential on the grounds of productivity and public health. It is already recognised that the provision of safe drinking water to low-income households constitutes a direct incentive for their enhanced socio-economic development.

The Government, with the involvement of stakeholders, must facilitate the rehabilitation of all water-borne sewage treatment systems in urban areas and must provide, where necessary, new water supply and sewage treatment systems.

Energy development policy

Zambia has great potential for generating hydro-electric power and the Government should facilitate the use of this cheaper, cleaner and environmentally friendly source of energy by more households.

Adequate management systems for wood-fuel must be put in place to conserve the use of wood, especially near urban areas. The problems of shrinking local wood-fuel supplies and the resulting deforestation and desertification of the environment around major urban settlements must be reversed for the sake of future generations.

More research and efforts must be put in place to develop and promote the use of sustainable sources of energy.

Transport development policy

The Government must formulate a sustainable transport policy with a view to maintaining adequate supply, standardisation of equipment, improving the quality of transport systems, and the co-ordination of transfer facilities between various modes. Maximum access to public transport, especially in rural areas and among the vulnerable groups, within high density housing areas and between settlements, must be given highest priority.

Appropriate institutional and legal frameworks must be put in place in order to promote adequate provision of transport for all and the accommodation of various transport modes, including pedestrians, cyclists and the handicapped, and the minimisation of mechanical, physical and psychological injury to travellers.

Road construction and maintenance programs should prioritise the construction of roads which are used by public transport and those leading to rural areas. The use of labour-intensive road construction and maintenance programs must be encouraged, especially on rural feeder road networks. This would not only provide additional employment opportunities and raise income levels, but also help to reduce poverty levels in rural areas.

Natural environment policy

Issues of pollution control and environmental conservation are subjects which require more focused attention in Zambia. The formulation of the National Conservation Strategy (NCS) by the Zambian Government in 1985, and the subsequent creation of the Environmental Council of Zambia (ECZ) are positive steps towards the sustainable development of human settlements and the natural environment in future.

National urbanisation policy

Human settlements do not operate in isolation. They exist as components of open global and national systems which are characterised by a rich lattice of environmental, economic and social interactions. In order to achieve urban sustainability, therefore, there is a need to harmonise urban and rural settlements' development patterns. Zambian towns and cities owe their present unsustainable development patterns largely to the continuing rural-urban migration waves. The present levels of rural-urban migration will only be reduced when the variety of shelter, employment opportunities and services which are found in cities and towns are developed in smaller towns and rural settlements, the present source of migrants.

The adoption and implementation of a national urbanisation policy based on the balanced socio-economic development of urban and rural settlements is, therefore, crucial to the sustainable development of Zambia's human settlements during the Twenty First Century.

Conclusion

The Zambian Government, through the formulation, adoption and implementation of a sustainable national urbanisation policy, must commit itself to the efficient use of all resources, under the market-led economic policy, in harmony with nature, fair play and justice to all, and in the interests of the present and future generations. This is the challenge which planners must meet in order to achieve the sustainable development of human settlements in Zambia.

Bibliography

Hardoy, J.E., Mitlin, D, and Satterthwaite, D.E. (eds.), (1987), *Environmental Problems in Third World Cities*, London: Earthscan.

International Union for the Conservation of Nature and Natural Resources (IUCN), (1980), *World Conservation Strategy: Living Resource Conservation for Sustainable Development*, Gland, Switzerland, IUCN-UNEP-WWF.

Katele, C.P, (1996), 'Best Practices In Community Infrastructure Development', *Mimeo.*, The Copperbelt University, Kitwe, 1995.

United Nations Commission for Environmental Development (UNCED), (1992), *Agenda 21*, Chapter 7, UN Publication Sales No.E92.1.1.

United Nations Commission on Human Settlements, (UNCHS-Habitat) January, (1995), *Sustainable Development in an Urbanising World, Including Issues Related to Land Policies and Mitigation of Natural Disasters*, Nairobi, HS/C/15/6, P.3.

Welbank, Michael, (1994), article in the *Town and Country Planning Summer School Proceedings*, Royal Town Planning Institute, London.

World Bank Report (WBR), (1994), No. 12985-ZA, Zambia: Poverty Assessment".

World Bank Tables (WBT), (1995), World Bank, Washington DC.

World Bank, (1995), *Social Indicators of Development* (WB/SIOD), World Bank, Washington DC.

World Commission on Environment and Development.(WCED), (1987), *Our Common Future*, Oxford, Oxford University Press.

World Development Report (WDR), (1980), World Bank, Washington DC.

World Development Report (WDR), (1992), World Bank, Washington DC.

World Development Report (WDR), (1994), World Bank, Washington DC.

Zambia, Government of the Republic of, Central Statistical Office (GRZ/CSO), (1980), *Census of Population and Housing*, Vol. II", Government Printer, Lusaka.

Zambia, Government of the Republic of, Central Statistical Office, (GRZ/CSO/CPHA), (1990), CSO, *Census of Population, Housing and Agriculture* and *Priority Survey II*, (1993), Government Printer, Lusaka.

Zambia, Government of the Republic of, National Commission for Development Planning (GRZ/NCDP), (1995), *Economic Report*, (1995) Government Printer, Lusaka.

Zambia, Government of the Republic of, National Commission for Development Planning (GRZ/NCDP/FONDP), (1988), *Fourth National Development Plan*, (1989-1993), Government Printer, Lusaka.

Zambia, Government of the Republic of (GRZ/CSO:NASB), January,(1990), *National Accounts Statistical Bulletin No.3 of 1990* , Central Statistical Office, Government Printer, Lusaka.

Zambia, Government of the Republic of, Central Statistical Office (GRZ/CSO:NASB), January, (1992), *National Accounts Statistical Bulletin No. 4 of (1992)*, Central Statistical Office, Government Printer, Lusaka.

Zambia, Government of the Republic of, Ministry of Local Government and Housing (GRZ/MLGH), (1996), *National Housing Policy*, Government Printer, Lusaka.

Zambia, Government of the Republic of, Central Statistical Office (GRZ/CSO), (1990), *Preliminary Report, Census of Population, Housing and Agriculture*, Government Printer, Lusaka.

Zambia, Government of the Republic of, Central Statistical Office (GRZ/CSO:PS), *Priority Survey II*, (1993), Lusaka.

Zambia, Government of the Republic of, (1995) *Government Paper No.1 of (1995)*, Government Printer, Lusaka.

Zambia, Government of the Republic of, National Commission for Development Planning (GRZ/NCDP:PIP), (1995), *Public Investment Programmes (1995-1997)* Government Printer, Lusaka.

Zulu, ALM, *Key Housing Indicators for Zambia*, (1995), National Housing Authority, Lusaka.

8 Economic and social consequences of managerial reforms of the health industry in Zambia

Herrick C Mpuku

Introduction

Following recent political changes in Zambia, the government enunciated policy reforms in the health industry, with particular reference to the publicly-funded health sector. These reforms involve a major reorganisation of the industry in line with the dominant liberal philosophy of the government.

The new policy pronouncements include *inter alia*, the introduction of a fee-paying system in place of the old free access medical system, and a departure from the centrally-administered and centrally-funded system of administering government hospitals and other health facilities. In addition, the government liberalised the health industry, in general, by permitting the establishment of full-fledged hospitals by private individuals and organisations to supplement or compete with existing public health facilities, as the case may be.

It will become evident that, with the collapse of the previous government's heroic efforts to provide free medical care to its population throughout its hospitals as demonstrated by the prolonged shortage of medical personnel, drugs and other related facilities, it has become imperative to have a fresh look at the management, administration and financing of health care if improvements are to be effected for the benefit of the community.

Such a review, and the institution of appropriate remedial measures, such as the provision of administrative and financial autonomy, organisational restructuring, introduction of user fees, increased use of commercial principles in health management, and the liberal policy environment, would be expected to resuscitate the health care institutions and ensure that they provide a reasonable level of medical care to the population.

It is obvious that the reforms may have positive effects, in giving a new lease of life to medical services, but would also adversely affect the population, particularly the low income groups as the presumed ready access to various medical facilities will become severely circumscribed under the new regime.

In addition, the success of the reforms will depend on the capacity of the newly- transformed institutions to manage the transition to, and sustenance of the new systems of health management, and the regulatory and policy framework of health services to widen access to medical care, assure quality and protect patient interests.

The objective of this paper is to provide a preliminary evaluation of the reforms being undertaken, and to assess the capacity and prospects of the institutions to provide good quality medical care so that the greatest number of people benefit from health services; appropriate measures are suggested in an effort to strengthen health care delivery to the public.

The paper will examine the background to the development of the health industry and the guiding philosophy. The philosophy, principles, practice and proposed plans of the new health reforms will subsequently be outlined. The transition to a new system of medical care are informed by recent conceptual and policy debates on the subject. We then examine the constraints on the attainment of the objectives of reforms given recent surveys of hospitals and other research. The policy implications of these findings are indicated and appropriate recommendations are put forward.

The basis of this study is a review of the management literature in relation to the published performance, policies and practices of the health sector.

These are supported by interviews of various professional cadres in the health establishment.

Background to health industry and health reforms

History

The evolution of health care in Zambia, and Africa in general, can be traced from the traditional healers to the coming of missionaries, and various forms of intervention by public and private sector interventions in the provision of both general and exclusive health care. Schram (1985) has outlined this evolution showing how various missionary groups and individuals contributed to the development of health care in Africa, through research and practice in the various health centres established throughout Africa.

Through such efforts and their collaboration with the medical establishment in Europe, it was possible to identify and develop treatments for such illnesses as malaria and sleeping sickness, create a base for training and developing health cadres in nursing, midwifery and other forms of medical care and establish non-traditional medical practices as an important and essential feature of health care in Africa. The efforts in research and medical care by the missionaries were also supplemented by colonial governments involvement in the field which set up health and research centres, meant to support their administrative and military staff in the colonies. These included organisations like the French SGHMP which provided surveillance, detection and treatment of such diseases as smallpox, malaria, meningitis, leprosy, schistosomiasis and trachoma, among others.

The growing urbanisation of Africa created new public health problems, and required the active involvement of commercial and industrial interests to preserve the health of their workers. In the mining areas, for instance, the incidences of pneumonia, pneumoconiosis and tuberculosis increased as a result of poor working and crowded living conditions. Venereal diseases, alcoholism and violence also increased especially given disruptive social effects of urbanisation. It was, therefore, necessary for the mining companies to take an active interest in the health care facilities as a way of protecting the health and productivity of their employees.

At the time of independence, many governments felt they had to intervene positively to stimulate the rapid growth of the health sector in the interests of the population at large. This intervention took the form of the creation of state hospitals and health centres, the development of health training institutions and related teaching hospitals for doctors, nurses and other medical support staff (medical assistants, laboratory assistants, etc.). Many of the state hospitals, as in Zambia, were made free to the public in line with the ideology and government policy of equal access for all to medical facilities.

Thus a two-tier health system was created in which the free-state hospitals operated side-by-side with private hospitals and nursing homes.

Post independence policies in Zambia

Undoubtedly, the governments health policy as many other social sector policies, were motivated by ideological considerations of social equality and access for all. Subsequently, and in the same spirit, the government decided to discontinue the fee-paying private health services which were considered to be 'elitist'. All health facilities were to administered by the government, with lesser control and assistance being exercised and provided to mission hospitals in different parts of the country. The policy of government yielded dividends in the sense that was a rapid expansion of health facilities in terms of hospitals, health centres and training institutions from 1964 to 1980.

The only private health facilities which were permitted, and continued to operate albeit at a small level of consultation, basic examination and prescription, were the private surgeries run by very few doctors. There was no provision in these facilities for admissions, X-rays, surgery and other sophisticated forms of medical care. In the event of serious conditions, these patients could be referred to the larger government or government-aided missionary hospitals for further medical attention.

However, over a period of time and in the light of growing problems of access to public health facilities, many private and parastatal companies began to develop their own private health facilities, singly and in-house or in collaboration with existing private practitioners. Others like the giant state-owned mining companies developed fullfledged industrial hospitals for the exclusive use of their employees in the event of work-related accidents or any other form of infirmities which might arise.

The state of public health services; 1980-1991

The policy of the colonial government, and the subsequent active involvement of post independence government led to the rapid development of a massive infrastructure rendering such services across the country.

Three major levels of hospital facilities can be identified in this regard; at district level, there are district hospitals, all provincial centres have general hospitals. The major Copperbelt towns of Ndola and Kitwe have Central hospitals servicing communities beyond their immediate vicinity, while Lusaka, the capital city, has an elaborate teaching hospital linked to the University of Zambia's School of Medicine.

In addition to these, one finds specialised hospitals such as the Chainama (Psychiatric) hospital in Lusaka, and the Arthur Davison (children's) hospital in Ndola; Health Centres and other specialised and general clinics are found widely across the rural and urban areas. Most of these institutions were able to provide reasonable level of service so long as the government was about to sustain them through continued funding for personnel, equipment, drugs and general development.

However, the onset of the Zambian economic crisis in the early 1970s, increasingly brought the governments health policy under pressure, and inevitably into question. Dwindling government revenue meant that the government could not maintain the real growth in expenditure which was essential to ensure the provision of a good quality of medical care. According to the national health policy document (GRZ, 1992, p.7) expenditure on health declined by almost 30% in real terms between 1981 and 1991.

The declining level of resource allocation to the health establishment coupled with foreign exchange and other macroeconomic problems resulted in shortages of drugs, limited availability of new equipment and poor maintenance of old equipment as well as stunted development. The exodus of staff to private and parastatal companies and abroad as a result of relatively poor conditions of service in government severely weakened the government's ability to sustain the state hospital system. As at 1991, only half of the doctors' establishment was filled, and only a quarter for dentists (GRZ, 1992, p.12). The public health sector was thus heavily dependent on clinical offers (80% of establishment filled), registered and enrolled nurses

(40% and 80% in excess of establishment) as well as other junior medical personnel. (See National Health Policy document, 1992, for table).

In all, there was a general decline in health services with limited accessibility to qualified medical personnel for treatment, poor availability of drugs, overcrowded hospitals with poor equipment such as beds, and beddings, as well as medical monitoring equipment. With this trend being the norm in most public hospitals across the country, it was self evident that the government's health policy was not only in crisis but had clearly failed. Public hospitals could no longer be relied on as purveyors of free, if any, medical services at all (GRZ, 1992, pp. 59-60).

The intensified economic hardships for health workers, against a background of general decline in hospital standards began to weaken the strong code of professionalism that exists in the medical corps; industrial actions in the form of go-slows and all-out strikes intermittently occurred in the hospital system while the senior grades of medical personnel (doctors), which are meant to provide expert opinion and guidance on treatment, training of, and research by junior medical staff, became thinner and thinner. The management of the health facility had clearly shifted to inexperienced and/or unqualified staff raising serious doubts about the credibility and integrity of the health facility.

Many junior doctors interviewed complained about the small number of senior medical staff, which limited access to expert and experienced personnel to provide them with such guidance and training.

In addition, they cite poor equipment (such as absence of ultrasound, EEG, etc.), poor working conditions and environment which removed the challenge associated with the profession.

The low pay which was linked to civil service administrative scale, and barely reflected the professionalism inherent in medical training and care, was an important demotivating factor leading to the high level of attrition of staff to other sectors of the economy which were more rewarding. The differential between the benefits in public hospitals and the industrial hospitals, could be of the order of 300-400%, to the extent that the full range of benefits can be accurately assessed, (car, house, loans, allowances etc.), and considerably higher when compared with similar institutions in the region.

The centralised system of selection, promotion and discipline of staff inevitably meant that there was a great deal of inefficiency in appointments and provision of relevant conditions of service. It was also not possible to maintain high standards of discipline at work since disciplinary procedures were governed by civil service general order, which were unduly elaborate requiring even cases of very junior staff to be referred to the Ministry of Health headquarters in Lusaka. Clearly, incentives for high and consistent work standards and professionalism in the management of the health services were lacking. The inability to make important local and urgent decisions for managers simply impairs their capacity to manage effectively.

The lack of drugs, which situation had been exacerbated by the central buying and allocation system through Medical Stores Limited and the Ministry of Health meant that hospitals frequently ran out of essential drugs leaving them in a position of utter helplessness vis-à-vis the patient; nothing can be more frustrating to a medical professional than failing to save a life because of the absence of basic drugs and equipment.

Mwanawina (1993, p.75) reports on the decline in health service citing the case of the country's largest hospital the UTH which had few beds and beddings, no running water, no steam for sterilisation and general poor sanitation in the hospital, in addition many of the operating theatres were closed together with specialised clinics and some general hospitals elsewhere in the country.

The general malaise in the health service was a nation-wide phenomenon which had serious socioeconomic consequences, with mortality increasing rapidly especially from such diseases as malaria, respiratory diseases and, latterly, cholera and meningitis (CSO, 1987, GRZ, 1986, GRZ, 1983). The death toll from cholera and meningitis in the 1989-92 period in the urban area was shockingly high. This was a reflection of a serious decline in the socio-economic and living conditions of the population and the collapse of public health facilities meant to provide early warning for preventive action.

Though the government of the day recognised the serious and unacceptable state of the health service and the need for reform, it was clear they were ideologically constrained and lacked the vision and political will to initiate radical measures to save the health service. Consequently, the half-hearted measures to introduce administrative reform and user fees were fraught with failure.

It was against this background, that the new government opted for a departure from existing health policies and chose to reorganise the entire public health system, altering its capacity and accessibility by the general public (GRZ, 1992).

This obviously raises serious questions about possible direction and the philosophy of future health policy for developing countries, and Zambia, in particular. The central issue remains that of how to ensure that a cost effective and possibly self-sustaining health system provides good quality health care to as many people as possible.

Whither health policy; some conceptual and policy issues

The design of health policy and health care systems has been the subject of discussion for a long time and these have been coloured by the ideological view point of protagonists; the choice between free health care and fee-paying; whether patients should pay for health services through taxes or directly for specific services rendered. And what happens to those who cannot afford?

It has been suggested that health should be the entitlement of all members of the community, whether rich or poor. Pepper (1983) cites US court cases which oblige the state to support those who cannot fend for themselves. A court ruling in California said (p.39):

> It has never been, nor will it ever be, questioned that among the first or primary duties evolving upon the State is that of providing suitable means and measures for the proper care and treatment, at the public expense of the indigent sick, having no relatives legally liable for their care.

Such a ruling establishes a case for public support of the vulnerable groups in society. Though it does not specify who is indigent or the means of identifying them. It does, nevertheless, clearly suggest that health should be accessible to all. It devolves to the State to derive fit and proper means to ensure that all sections of the population have access to health care, and are not disadvantaged by their economic status. The design of the health care system as an expression of such public policy, therefore, becomes important.

The World Bank Conference on Development (1992) debated the roles and responsibilities of governments and individual members of the community in the maintenance of public health. Some contributors identified the role of the State as against the private sector as that of, *inter alia*, developing and complementing health plans and policies, ensuring acceptable and accessible health care to the population not covered by private health services and ensuring a standard of care compatible with resource availability; in addition the State should also be involved in gathering and distributing information for planning and creating a healthy environment and co-ordinating donor contributions to the health sector

The private health sector, on the other hand, should supplement the public sector by providing services to private individuals, "improving efficiency and the quality of health care by fostering competition, and supplying, some services the public sector cannot afford such as radiotherapy, computerised tomography (CT) scans and other high technology services". (World Bank, 1992, p. 44).

Others, however, have disputed whether it is prudent to distinguish between the private and public sector in this way. Drawing such a distinction, in their view, oversimplifies the debate and detracts from a creative mix of the two which is likely to assure better delivery of health care in the future.

However, the essential principle of drawing some dichotomy is sustained because private sectors activities, in the quest for profits are not always likely to produce health. The government should as a matter of national interest, invest in that range of interventions that were likely to do so. These included socio-medical research, preventative medicine and economic disincentives for non-health producing activities (e.g. tax on smoking, alcohol etc.), immunisation and health education etc. These, according to the World Bank report (1993 a, b) were more likely to constitute a more cost-effective use of public resources for health purposes.

One of the general conclusions emanating from this debate is that the health care system must be a two or three tier system in which the majority of the people would be served by the bottom tier. At this level, health care would be served as a public good and would, therefore, be publicly financed (or through public insurance). The upper tier would cater for the rich and would provide exclusive privately financed (or private insurance) facilities not necessarily essential for health care, and if *such* "people wanted to buy unnecessary operations that might kill them (then) that would be their problem" (p.416).

There can, therefore, be a role for the private sector, the public and the patient in making health services available. A careful consideration of socio-economic factors is, therefore, essential in order to make for a creative combination of the three players to allow for optimal delivery of health care to the public. At very low levels of per capita income, it is necessary for extreme caution to be exercised in the implementation of such new policies, which may have a telling effect on the majority of the populace.

Health reforms: principles and practices

The health reforms mooted in the health policy document (GRZ, 1992) is the most comprehensive health review package in a very long time. Essentially, it reverses the previous government's policy of free medical care which could not be financially sustained and eventually resulted in a virtual collapse of the public health system. The fee-paying system which has been introduced aims at achieving some form of cost-sharing and allows the individual members of the public to bear some responsibility for their health without the government necessarily abrogating its obligations for the maintenance of public health.

The enabling policy framework (GRZ, 1985, 1992) passed to support the new arrangement is a more complete and courageous version of the policy enunciated earlier by the previous government as exemplified by the creation of the Management Board of the University Teaching Hospital in 1985. The new legislation permits the creation of autonomous Health Management Boards for all the major hospitals and districts in Zambia. The new system of management permits these Boards to set their own fees (for consultancy and prescriptions,) determine conditions of service for staff and engage in any other developments of the hospitals and health services for which they are responsible. (An instance of similar boards includes the Irish Republic, Hensey, 1979).

In addition, the central role of government in the day-to-day administration of hospitals and health centres is being revised with the abolition of the Directorate of Medical Services nested in the Ministry of Health and its substitution thereof by the Central Board of Health, with its secretariat held by the Ministry of Health. The role of the Ministry headquarters, which will hold the secretariat of the CBH will be reduced to that of policy generation, formulation and supervision, (GRZ, 1992) while the Central Board of Health will monitor, integrate and co-ordinate the activities of the different health boards throughout the country to ensure that these are consistent with national health policy.

The Central Board of Health (CBH) is not specifically mentioned in the policy document, though it has been suggested in the public pronouncements of policy makers. There is mention of a National Health Council which duplicates the stated functions of the CBH, though looser in definition than the latter. The structure of the Boards with their emphasis on public representation effectively shifts the responsibility of health services to community and individual efforts, as these will now have the power to influence administration and development of their respective services.

Contraints on health reforms

User fees and value of services

The major policy change of profound public concern is the introduction of user fees on medical services. The fear that has been expressed in many quarters is that the great majority of people would not be in a position to meet the expenses of otherwise essential medical services and will, therefore, go without. This would be expected to apply as a general rule for most people especially in an era of rapidly declining real incomes, unexpected or emergency cases of illness for others; Initially, those those who could not afford were turned away, though, there has been some progress in providing access since then. In a country where personal expenditure on health services has historically been very low (C.S.O. 1977), the adjustment to the new situation cannot be easy.

While policy makers recognise some of the difficulties that people may face in this regard, it is felt that some of the fears expressed may have been exaggerated, and may be largely an overhang of the past culture of free medical services. It has, for instance, been suggested that a lot of people undertake to seek consultation and treatment from traditional healers and private non-traditional health practitioners, who charge a fee for their services; why then should they not pay other medical services?

One might also consider that perhaps taxation of people may be the basis of providing "free" health care. However, in a society were informality is high and the taxation system is not very well developed, it is almost inevitable, and is a truism, that the burden of taxation impacts heavily only on a small section of the population in formal sector employment who may not necessary have higher incomes than their counterparts in the non-formal sector or make greater use of health services than the others. It is evident then that formal sector employees would bankroll the "free" health sector and subsidise the rest of the untaxed users. Such a system is clearly inequitable.

It should be clear that all health services have a cost, and the point at issue would be to determine or allocate that cost as equitably as possible taking into account the usage of facilities and capacity to pay. Health is both a public good and a private good. While individuals may wish to avoid the inconvenience of ill-health or enhance their wellness at a personal level, through appropriate treatments, it is possible that lack of treatment or appropriate health education may result in generalised illnesses in the form of epidemic, endemic and pandemic diseases. Such a situation with its concomitant effects on loss of man-days and, possibly, skills in the event of death, would have deleterious effects on production and productivity as well as the society's economic well-being. Thus both the government and the individuals must play their role to ensure successful health care provision in the society.

While the principle of payment for services in one form or another has a plausible argument in its favour, the practical problem of determining an appropriate fee becomes important. First, the efficient organisation, of the health facility, which has hitherto not been the case is essential if patients are to meet legitimate expenses and avoid questionable overheads (World Bank, 1993a, p.12). This is particularly important in a case were the public health sector and related institutions loom large, and do not face any significant competition from other health facilities, especially in the transition. Wide public consultation on, as well as policing and regulation of costing and pricing practices may be necessary to avoid abuse and assure fairness in price determination.

Secondly, the asymmetry in medical information between the patient and the health care provider may lead the latter to over-prescribe treatment, which may not be necessary and which the patient would not choose if he knew better. Unnecessary or wrong drugs, unduly long admissions and so on, can increase the cost of health care to the patient, without improving, and possibly adversely affecting, the health of the patient.

Third, and closely related to the above, there is need to ensure value of money; that is, patients must get the treatment that they pay for. This requires some form of assurance of quality or code of practice to guide patient expectations and medical officer's practice. This might also entail a change in patient-doctor relations in which the patient ceases to be a passive recipient of whatever drugs the doctor considers expedient. The patient must play an active role in his own treatment with the doctor fully explaining the nature and implication of the treatment provided. The patient can make known his concerns and should be fully aware of the scope of treatment. Medicine, as a field of study has its limits, and medical practitioners, will have their own individual limitations. Patients must be conscious of these, as well as their rights, and obligations in their relationship with the medical practitioner.

Management and strategy

It is also useful to consider that the health system is in transition from an archaic system of administration. The management system and the staff have operated under a system of limited sensitivity to consumers or patient interests, especially in circumstances of limited and declining health services. Moreover, medical staff have not been trained in the now pertinent areas of management, finance, customer relations and the intricacies of value for money and value of life. It remains to be seen whether the organisational culture of the civil service/monopoly and pay system can be transformed to one where the patient is central and determines the success of health practitioners. Clearly, the levels of reorganisation, reorientation and training will be quite demanding.

It has been indicated already that most of the health institutions have been operating under civil service conditions, in circumstances of declining health service standards, limited patient care and falling professionalism. In the adjustment phase, established practices and attitudes are difficult to reform, especially if these involve a major change in behaviour. This applies equally at both the management and operational levels.

It is essential that in the creation of an enabling external environment, efforts are made to substantially alter the internal system to allow consistent motivation of staff, and the appropriate reinforcement of evolving positive work attitudes of all staff. Such changes could take a long time, and the absence of vision, consistency and persistence could undermine efforts to accomplish and cement such changes.

At the top management level, the Board is expected to provide leadership and a strategic vision for their respective institution. In the conduct of its activities, such Boards must exercise appropriate autonomy without undue fear of unnecessary political interference. The security of tenure of office must be guaranteed except in the event of clear violation of national policy, legislation and regulations.

The method of selection of the Boards must also be such that they fully reflect the community interests that are served by the health facility; that is, those who have to pay fees, those who benefit or lose out, as the case may be, from changes in health services. The promotion of community involvement, especially at the Board level is the surest way to ensure sensitivity of management and staff to patient interests, as well as sustaining the interests of individual members of the community in the performance of their health services. There must, therefore, be an effort to involve the community at all levels of health service management whether as a patient, Board member or community member interested in the health service and its operations.

The tendency in many parastatal organisations where the selection of Board members is not transparent is not helpful; neither would it be appropriate to place too much emphasis on health service professionals in Board membership, as this runs the risk of losing sight of the need to focus on community service rather than merely serving the interests of professionals and workers at the expense of the customer as many organisations are wont to do.

For the same reason, senior managers need not necessarily be medical staff. In a transformational phase, requiring resource mobilisation and allocation, the stimulation of the work force and the creation of a policy-constrained enterprise, requires individuals with an understanding of strategic and operational management and an appreciation of the role of such institutions in provision of care in an heterogeneous community.

Policy implications and recommendations

In the foregoing review of the prospects of the Zambian Health service, we have identified a variety of management, administrative and financial bottlenecks, and have hinted at possible solutions. Here we present some of the implications of our findings and related recommendations.

Organisational structure

It has been argued in the literature (Chandler 1962; Ansoff, 1968) that strategy determines the structure of the organisation. It is also a common precept of strategic management that it is inevitable that as the environment changes, the corresponding strategy has to change; an appropriate structure to ensure the successful implementation of the strategy in a changing environment is therefore, inevitable.

We have already pointed out that the previous arrangement was essentially a civil service bureaucracy created as a time when resources were abundant. With changes in the environment, philosophy and policy, the internal institutional problems became more acute. Issues of professionalism, ranking and motivation are put forward by the different professional cadres and become more pressing, more urgent. How does one for instance determine the relative worth of doctors, nurses, clinical officers and paramedics?

Most of these issues can only be meaningfully determined with a comprehensive job evaluation of the health institutions. Nevertheless, it is useful to point out that in the determination of structure, it is essential to be mindful of the mission goals and strategy of the institution, and the key players in the fulfilment of these.

Once an institution decides what it is, why it was created and where it wishes to be in the long term as well as the related priorities, the relative worth and the reporting relationships between different professional cadres can be more easily determined. It also becomes possible to develop meaningful career structures for each profession.

Compensation system

While relative pay levels can be adjusted in time with adjustments to the organisational structure cited in 6.1, it is also essential to examine the level and structure of pay to identify its motivational content. This must be designed in such a way that it encourages high work output in general, and willingness to serve under adverse conditions such as long hours, night shifts, on-calls etc. It must also reinforce the career structure and that people can relate their progress in their career with enhanced levels of compensation.

In general, pay levels must be inter-sectorally and internationally comparable to avoid the haemorrhage of skills and loss of investment in human capital critical to health care delivery, and the success of health reforms in particular.

Management development and staff training

It is therefore inevitable that (1) programmes of training workshops for doctors and nurses in the principles of management, finance, social work and customer relations are developed, especially those joining and health services at the start of their career; (2) training workshops in positive work attitudes and customer relations are enhanced and (3) formal programmes of training at local educational institutions (Certificate, Diploma, Degrees) in health services management and administration are developed to strengthen professionalism in hospital management in the country. Finally (4), it will also be of value to incorporate the elements of finance, management, social work an enlightened patient (customer) relations in established medical training programmes for doctors, nurses and other medical staff.

Health insurance

Since a lot of people are unlikely to be in a position to pay for medical services on demand, it is necessary to introduce a comprehensive system of health insurance to ensure that there is access for all with the payment of a fixed annual fee. Upon membership and reasonable determination of means, the state can decide at what level some form of state subsidisation will be necessary. People will have different capacities to afford, even health insurance, depending on their economic status, and it is, therefore, the responsibility of the state to ensure that these others have access to health care.

Nevertheless, as with all insurance schemes it will be necessary to effect safeguards against over-consumption of the health facility by patients and cost-escalation by medical practitioners.

The financial constraints on customers of the health service will continue to loom large, and affect the accessibility of members to the community health care. It is, therefore, inevitable for government and both public and private health institutions to devise imaginative ways of providing health care such as capitulation and health maintenance organisations to ease these financial constraints while guarding against cost-escalation and decline in standards (Fromer, 1983; World Bank, 1993).

An enabling environment

The reform of the public health sector must go hand in hand with a generalised transformation of the health industry in the country. The success of public sector reforms will be heavily influenced by corresponding reforms in other areas which impinge, or are likely to impinge on the operations of the former.

For instance, the introduction of some degree of competition in the health sector might stimulate an improvement in the quality of health services provided. To this end, government must seriously consider opening the mine industrial hospitals to the public. Access to these institutions may be through an on-demand fee or the health insurance suggested above.

Since the mine hospitals are the only other significant purveyors of health service, in the country, their contribution to health care improvement can be fairly substantial.

In addition, as much encouragement as possible must be given to private investors to set up private hospitals and nursing homes to widen the availability, choice and quality of health service. Appropriate private health insurance schemes to facilitate participation of more people in private health care facilities, should also be encouraged.

As more private hospitals evolve, the present arrangement of a two-tier public sector hospital for rich and poor should be abolished. Except as a transitional arrangement, there should be no discrimination in access to basic health care since everyone must have confidence that they have an equal chance of being cared for to the same degree as any other person without discrimination in terms of access to medical staff, drugs, space and other supporting facilities. The present arrangement seems philosophically and conceptually flawed, and practically unfair to the general populace.

However, as more (private) health institutions are established, the two-tier system can develop in which all essential health care for all, at a high standard is available from the public sector, while those wishing for special standards over and above what is really necessary for normal health care (such as colour television, gourmet food, etc.) can find exclusive privately-financed health-care facilities. Public resources are much better utilised if they are focused on the provision of a high standard of cost-effective basic health care for all rather than expensive, luxurious and non-productive services (in terms of generation of health) (see also Griffin (1991) on a similar point). While the luxury services may appear to generate income, they run the risk of crowding out the less-privileged, as they direct institutional attention and resources from the provision of basic and essential care.

One of the difficulties which is likely to arise in the delivery of health care to the patients from both the public and private sector will be that of monitoring and regulating the activities of the health care providers. The regulatory mechanism of government in developing countries, and Zambia in particular, has historically been weak; it is, therefore, unlikely that the regulatory mechanism would be any better without special consideration. There is need, therefore, to strengthen the system of determining and enforcing standards; viz., to monitor, inspect, process customer complaints and to have the authority and capacity to penalise erring medical practitioners to ensure medical ethics and quality for patients are maintained, as well as guard against malpractices, as well as overvaluation and overinvoicing in both the public and private sectors (Harrison and Greton, 1984, pp. 115-123). In this way, the emerging health sector system will be protected, and the confidence that people have in it will be upheld.

Conclusion

We have reviewed the evolution of the health care system and related institutions in Africa and Zambia particularly. We have identified the problem which arose from the original public Zambian health policy, which though well-meant, could not be sustained because of dwindling resources. Hence the reason why health services collapsed and the standards of public health also declined.

A comprehensive review of the health sector was, therefore, inevitable. This, however, raises questions of accessibility to the public of the evolving service and the management capacity of the changing institution to deliver appropriate services of a good standard. While the signs are hopeful, there is need to address the problems of management systems and managers in the health services for quality, consistency and ethics if health care is to be attained and maintained.

In general, the success of many economic and social policies will depend on the strengthening of the management capacity of public institution and government agencies, and the development of an effective regulatory framework to support both public and private institutions.

Bibliography

Ansoff, I H, (1968) *Corporate Strategy*, Penguin books, Middlesex.

Central Statistical Office (1986) *Country Profile, Zambia, 1985*, Central Statistical Office.

Chandler, A D, JR, (1962) *Strategy and Structure*, The MIT Press, Cambridge, Mass.

CSO (1977) *Household Budget Survey 1974/75*, CSO, Lusaka.

Fromer, M J, (1983) *Community Health Care and Nursing Process*, The C.V Mistry company, London.

Government of the Republic of Zambia, (GRZ) *Economic Report*, (1983,1987,1991) Office of the President, National Commission for Development Planning, Lusaka, 1984, 1988, 1992.

Griffin, Charles, (1991) 'Setting Health Priorities in Health Care in Developing Countries', *Finance and Development*, Vol.28, No.4.

GRZ, (1987) *Bulletin of Health statistics, 1985-1986, Major Health Trends, 1976-86*, Ministry of Health, Lusaka.

GRZ, (1992) *National Health Policies and Strategies (Health Reforms)* Ministry of Health, Lusaka.

GRZ (1985) *Medical Sevices Act* , National Assembly.

GRZ (1989) *The New Economic Recovery Programme; Fourth National Development Plan*, Vol. 1 National Commission for Development Planning, Lusaka.

Harrison, A and J. Greton, (eds.) (1984) *Health Care UK 1984: An economic, social and policy audit* CIPFA/Policy Journal, London.

Mwanawina, I (1993)'Zambia' in A Adepoju (ed.) *The Impact of Structural Adjustment on the population of Africa: The implications for Education, Health and Employment.* UNFPA/James Currey, London.

Schram, R (1985) 'A History of Community Health in Africa,' in Sofoluwe, G.O. and F.T Bennet: (eds.) *Principles and Practice of Community Health in Africa,* University Press, Ibadan Central Statistical Office (1985, 1987) Monthly Digest Statistics.

World Bank, (1992) Round Table discussion: (the health of the public:) A Public Responsibility, *Proceedings of the World Annual Conference of Development Economics,* 1992.

World Bank (1993) *World Development Report 1993*; Investing in health; IBRD/The World Bank, Washington. Executive Summary and Full report.

9 Managing public universities in Africa in the 1990s and beyond; the human aspect of the challenge with special reference to the Copperbelt University, Zambia

George K Simwinga

Introduction

The problems besetting African Universities today are wide and common. They range from student enrolment which is rising faster than the Universities' capacity to plan and accommodate them (Mwiria, 1991, p.1), to declining and, often, under-funding (AAU 1991, p.1). They also include, among other problems, issues of the relevance or irrelevance (Saint 1992, p.14) for the kind of education being offered in terms of national priority needs. This brief paper focuses its attention on the human aspect of the challenge. Specifically, the paper looks at the main pressure groups in the university which have and are likely to play a pivotal role in the management of public universities in the foreseeable future. In this regard, three strong interest groups have been identified which have greatly influenced the governance of African Universities and the Copperbelt University, in particular, in the past, which in my view will continue shaping the destiny of these universities for the remainder of this century. These are: the students, the non-academic members of staff and the academics. In treating this subject and based on the experience of the Copperbelt University, the paper looks at the demands and interests of each of these groups, vis-à-vis the capacity of the University to meet these demands. It is our considered view that given these demands and the capacity of universities to address the same, the challenge of University Administration will be one that should seek to ensure stability in the development of these institutions by striking an appropriate balance between the interests of these pressure groups and the capacity of these institutions of higher learning. The following section, therefore, highlights, first of all, areas of conflict and some salient demands often made by these interest groups in a university community and the Copperbelt University in particular.

The main pressure groups in the university and their interests

The students

This is a formidable interest group in the case of the Copperbelt University, this comprises approximately 2000 students. The actions and strategies of students across the continent in putting over their demands are often free, sometimes extreme (Omari, 1991, p.18) and some areas, totally unrestrained compared to those of the others in the Copperbelt University, for example, are represented by a Union called the Copperbelt University Students Union (COBUSU). This has largely been responsible for a series of university closures, class boycotts and other forms of disruptions to the normal operations of the Copperbelt University since its inception. The Students Union for example was to a large extent responsible for the resignation of the Copperbelt University's first Vice Chancellor and also played a significant role together with other student unions in Zambia in forcing, and bringing about, democratic change to the political system.

Their demands and actions sometimes, as previously stated, go beyond the confines of the university campus in the role they played in precipitating political change in Africa such as changing from a one party to a multi-party system of governance (Mwira 1992: p.6). Their demands on the universities however take various forms and dimensions including, to mention only a few, the following:

Welfare In most African universities, there have been frequent and sometimes violent protests over what students regard as bad, if not inadequate and expensive food served by the universities (N'Diri Therese Assie-Lumumba 1993, p.52). Many students for example in the Copperbelt

University have consequentially decided to boycott buying food from the University cafeteria and have, instead, resorted to cooking food for themselves in dormitories. The impact of such an action on the halls of residence in terms of wear and tear has been devastating, to say the least. The dormitories of the Copperbelt University were in the first place not designed to cater for cooking let alone the numbers of students that it currently accommodates. The damage to halls of residence and destruction to electrical installations in 1993 compelled Administration to enforce the rule that prohibited cooking in dormitories. This led to a very serious confrontation between the student body led by COBUSU and the Administration.

The crisis was only averted by the intervention of government following government's assessment of what it termed a somewhat volatile political situation prevailing in the country at the time. Other welfare related issues such as poor dormitory, recreational and unhygienic washroom facilities have often been cited as platforms for serious students protests culminating sometimes in class boycotts and other forms of disturbance.

University management Historically, the Students Unions in African universities have often viewed the University Administration particularly the Vice Chancellor as a "defender" of the interests of the Government at the expense of their own "genuine and legitimate" interests (Mwira, 1992, p.8). This position in Zambian universities was always reinforced by the fact that, until the University Act was repealed in 1992, the Head of state, who was also the Chancellor of both the Copperbelt University and the University of Zambia, appointed Senior Administrators including Vice Chancellors. It is therefore little surprising that such suspicions persisted. The 1992 University Act has since thrown open to competition all senior university posts including those of Vice Chancellor, Deputy Vice Chancellor, Registrar, Bursar and Deans, etc. The contention by Students Unions had always been that the University Administration have not only been imposed on universities in order to protect and foster government interests but that the Administrators have always been insensitive to the legitimate and genuine demands of students, and, worse still, the Administration was viewed as an oppressive force delighting in imposing punishment under the guise of discipline on innocent and defenceless students.

Thus any form of disciplinary measures, academic or otherwise taken against a student were viewed with suspicion and hostility. There was, for example, in the Copperbelt University in 1993, a case of two drunken students who insisted that the sentry on the campus gate should lift the cross bar (intended for controlling vehicular traffic) for them to enter the campus, in spite of the existence of a side walk foot gate. When the guard refused, they grabbed a baton from him and repeatedly hit him on the head occasioning a serious wound. When the students were disciplined for this, there were protests suggesting that the action by those students did not warrant disciplinary action against them.

Academic Student protests and demands in African universities though quite rare also take the form of academic complaints (Omari, 1991 p.38). There have been, for example, cases in the Copperbelt University from students regarding what they perceived as academic inexperience of some members of staff. Some students have complained that a number of their lecturers who only a while ago were their room-mates now stand in front of their classrooms with chalk in hand. There have also been complaints about shortage of textbooks and inadequate capacity of teaching aids such as computers. And there has also been, from time to time, complaints from students about the high number of failure in some courses implying that the standards are being exaggerated only to punish students.

The unionised workers

This is a fairly sizeable pressure group comprising nearly six hundred workers made up of, largely, unskilled low income workers. Because their work is largely supportive in nature, their conditions of service are comparatively less attractive to those of the academic staff. They are nevertheless a very vociferous pressure group. Their prime concern in working for the University is making a living by meeting the basic necessities of life such as food shelter and security. While the majority know and care less about who their employer is few appreciate the mission of a university.

The majority of their members, therefore, find it exceedingly difficult to understand why the university as their employer should continue spending large sums of money on "non-essential" items such as computers, laboratory equipment, library books and even recruiting the expensive expatriates, while at the same time claiming that the university does not have the money to pay for the basic needs of their own "deprived and exploited" low income workers. This group is, by and large, hostile if not quite unfriendly to the other two pressure groups in the university. They, for example, reacted quite sharply when the Government of Zambia under pressure granted a meal allowance of K1,000 a day to students which was also tax free. They resented the idea, arguing that the students were given a "take home pay" twice as much as they themselves get in addition to free tuition and board that they already enjoy.

The hostilities between the two groups is, however, mutual. If and when for example, the unionised workers go on strike, they receive little or no sympathy from students It is a common practice that when Unionised workers go on strike, the students are not only eager but do in fact volunteer to fill up the gap at little or no remuneration.

At the same time, the Unionised workers also find their relationship with academics somewhat lukewarm. They, for example, find it difficult to justify the disparity in salaries and other conditions of service between them and the academic members of staff. It is for this reason that each year during negotiations with management they take existing conditions of service of the academic staff as a bench mark. At a recent University Council meeting, the Labour Union Leader lamented why there should be a differential in holiday and bereavement allowances between unionised workers and academics. There remarks were not welcome by the representative of the academic staff.

The inter-group differences and jealousies aside, the Unionised workers are a formidable group in the life of the University. They constitute a sizeable work force since, as in may universities in developing countries, the Copperbelt University cannot afford capital intensive techniques in doing support jobs and, therefore, has to rely largely on labour. The unionised workers use the strike action as the most powerful tool to extract concessions, or draw attention to their demands. In some cases the use of industrial sabotage against the employer which includes among other dirty tactics manipulation of facts and realities including outright dis-information about the institution. There have been for example in the Copperbelt University cases where anonymous letters have been sent to the Investigator General and recently to the Chancellor giving complete fabrications about some senior officers of the university. It is therefore important to recognise the role and place of this particular group, their fears, their interests and the strategies they use in articulating their demands, if appropriate governance has to be achieved in a university.

The academic members of staff

This group is the 'cradle' and indeed essence of a university from the human resource point of view. The other categories of staff though important are only supportive. Few people opt for academic life simply as a way of making a living or as an alternative employment. Universities, particularly in developing countries have not been known to be the best employers in terms of the attractiveness of the conditions of service considering the type of talent offered.

Many academics join universities because of the perceived "self satisfaction" they expect from the job, and their commitment to academic and research pursuits. This unfortunately later turns out to be done at the expense of personal and family interests. The individual academic and indeed, his family ultimately find themselves deprived of the essentials in life which are enjoyed and often taken for granted by contemporaries who opted for life in either commerce or industry.

In a number of cases, some academics have in consequence succumbed to pressure and given up their academic careers to take up more remunerative jobs elsewhere. This has resulted in universities experiencing high levels of turnover of highly qualified and experienced talent. Those that have held on to their commitment to university life have been forced by economic circumstances to divide up their time between university work and "moonlighting" to supplement family incomes. This had tended to adversely affect the required time for research and teaching.

At the Copperbelt University, one of the recent developments has been a tendency by some academic members of staff to spend quite a proportion of their time in consultancy and the running of short seminars in collaboration with industry which are tailored around specific target groups. These activities pay them well and within a short period of time. Besides, incomes from these jobs are usually tax free. The effect of this on the university is that if not properly monitored, less time would be devoted to teaching and the required attention to individual students lost. It would also tend to interfere with individual lecturer's attention to research and publication of their own work - a cardinal ingredient to academic advancement in a university.

Other areas of concern that have contributed to the exodus of academics from African universities include the inability of universities to provide life long security to their members of staff such as the "Home-Ownership" and

"Car-Loan" schemes (Mwiria, 1992, p.8). It is for example common to find a university professor who has faithfully served a university for over twenty years with neither a house of his own or a simple personal car. At the Copperbelt University for example, year after year we have encountered great difficulty in persuading the central government which is our principal source of income to give us adequate 'seed money' to start both the 'home-ownership' and the 'car loan' schemes. This has caused great anxiety and helplessness to the University Administration as well as great frustration to the Academics, the intended beneficiaries of these schemes, who often see their former students hardly a year or two after leaving the university owning houses and driving cars of their own.

Other areas causing great disenchantment among academics include what is perceived as exclusion from the decision-making process in the running of the university (Mwira, 1992, p.8). The traditional university structures tend to deny long serving academics who do not hold leadership posts access to critical decision making points. In most cases, they have to speak only through a series of representatives such as departmental heads, Deans or Academic Association representatives. In the process their impact in influencing decision making is diminished causing, in consequence, great frustration. We have also had several complaints like in other African universities from senior academics about how they feel left out in major decisions affecting the running of the university (Saint, 1992, p.73). In some cases, this has made them withdraw their support for new initiatives in the university.

The human aspect of the challenge in managing public universities in the 1990s and beyond

In the preceding section, we have highlighted only a few areas of grievances as often articulated by the major interest groups in a university in a developing country and the Copperbelt University, in particular. Some of these concerns are admittedly shared. For example, the home ownership and car loan schemes as a concern attributed to academics are of equal interests to the Unionised workers. In this section rather than discuss remedies to these problems according to each interest group, we shall attempt to prescribe only in general terms what needs to be done when dealing with human resource factors in managing a public university during the remaining part of this century and beyond, in order to ensure stability and good governance.

Treating grievances seriously

The starting point in our view in managing the human resource is to recognise, attend to, and squarely address the group as much and as earnestly as you can within the means and capacity of the university. If and when no solution to the demand is possible (as is likely to be the case sometimes), it is incumbent upon the administration to explain to the parties concerned the inability of the university to do so.

Democratise decision making

Representation By widening and including representatives of all the major, critical and appropriate interest groups on key governing bodies such as Senate and Council. This should also be extended to those decision making organs of the university which impacts on the lives of various interest groups. For example, representatives from the Academic Association, the Unionised workers should be included on Tender Boards, Housing Committee, Loan Committee and Staff Welfare Committee etc. A Vice Chancellor's Advisory Board should also embrace representatives from various interest groups of the university community.

Making critical administrative posts elective All critical decision making posts including those of the Vice Chancellor, Deputy Vice Chancellor, Registrar, Bursar, Deans, Heads of departments and units must be opened to competition to all eligible candidates. At the Copperbelt University the posts of Deans are elective. The 1992 University Act provides for the appointment of the Vice Chancellor, his Deputy, the Registrar etc. by a non Head of State Chancellor (who is not the Head of State) on the recommendation of the University Council following an assessment of candidates who had been interviewed for the post by a Committee appointed by the University Council. Hitherto, a Vice Chancellor was appointed by the Head of State who was also the Chancellor of the University.

Promote and encourage dialogue between administration and
the various interest groups in the university

The following mechanisms can be employed to promote dialogue between
the various groups.

(a) Instituting a system of regular contacts and consultations. It is
important to institute a system of regular contacts and consultations between
the Administration on one hand and all the various constituent interest
groups on the other. This could be done through regular formal and informal
contacts. This approach would not only enable the Administration to
understand grievances and also solicit ideas, but it would also facilitate
diffusing potentially explosive situations before they happen.

(b) Encouraging and promoting communication through information
flow between the Administration on one hand and all the other constituent
interest groups on the other, through for example, the print media such as
"In-house" newsletter. Other additional and useful media of enhancing
communication should include holding regular policy briefing meetings on
various interest groups at which university policies and planned actions could
be explained. These are also the appropriate fora at which University
Council's decisions and indeed government policies as they affect the
university could be explained. In the Copperbelt University, for example, a
beginning has been made in this regard. Occasional meetings with the
principle pressure groups are held either at the request of the Administration
or the request of interest groups themselves.

(c) Encouraging and Strengthening staff and student Unions and
Associations, since strong Unions and Associations representing various
interest groups are an asset to the Administration, as they provide a
formidable buffer between the individual members of various interest groups
and Administration. They also serve as an early warning system for the
Administration which provides an opportunity to the Administration to begin
looking for solutions to a looming danger. It is easier and more effective to
deal with a strong united and respected body representing an interest group
within the university. An agreement with such representatives is in itself a
deal with the entire membership of interest group which they represent. On
the other hand, a weak and fragmented Union Leadership often finds their
agreement with the Administration thrown out and the entire team branded

'sell-outs'. This puts the clock backwards as the Administration suddenly finds itself looking for another representative to work with or else they have to find a way of bargaining with hundreds of individual employees at a time.

Scarce financial resources to support the needs of the human resource

The success of ensuring good governance in managing universities will depend to a large measure on how well the Administration meets the basic needs of the various interest groups. In each of the cases we have dealt with, part of the problem lies in the universities inability to meet the basic needs be it student welfare, adequate salaries and conditions of service of both the Academic and Unionised workers and the exodus of academics.

It is, therefore, one of the principle challenges and requirements of successfully managing universities to find adequate financial resources to support the needs of the various interest groups that constitute the university community. In the past decade universities in Africa, at least those in Zambia, have experienced a steadily declining level of financial support from the central governments which in fact are the main financiers of these institutions.

Coupled with this has also been the recent development from the international community which has shifted its education support priorities from financing tertiary education in support of primary education. The net result has been that universities have found themselves unable to improve on both the quality and size of their educational programmes. They have failed to maintain let alone rehabilitate existing infrastructure. Improvements to salaries and conditions of service to their staff has been a far cry.

It is therefore imperative that those who run universities have to devise if not find effective ways of persuading national governments to allocate more an adequate financial resources to universities in order to sustain both expansion and improvements to the quality education being offered, as ell as to adequately cater for the demands of the various constituent interests groups in the university. While it is recognised that there are now rising competing demands on the national cake as nationals increasingly become aware of their rights, it is wrong for national governments to abdicate their responsibilities regarding the education of their citizens. Even developed countries continue allocating a sizeable portion of the national budget to education.

The international donor agencies too have over-stretched their policy reversal to the eventual detriment of the education system as a whole in developing countries. While accepting that primary education is indeed a basic human right, assuming this to be the underlying philosophy of this policy shift, they have to realise that , if universities do not produce teachers, there will be no primary schools in the end. Universities working in collaboration with national governments must, therefore, find ways of appealing to and persuading the international donor community to review this policy which to a large measure in its present forms is retrogressive.

Finally, universities themselves should strive to embark on income generating ventures to supplement the new dwindling resources from the traditional sources. This, obviously has to be done cautiously bearing in mind that in their zeal to reduce total financial dependence on government, the basic mission of the university is not lost. But it is important that the universities should strive to raise funds to help out in place programmes that are vulnerable to the annual government cuts and also to help supplement the basic needs of the members of staff if and when the government and international donor agencies refuse to grant the universities the funds that they request.

Conclusion

In this paper it has been argued that one of the challenges in managing universities during the remainder of this century will be the handling of the human resource that constitute various interest groups in the university. Demands of the three main pressure groups namely the students, the Unionised workers and the academics, have been highlighted in so far as they affect and influence university governance. The paper has suggested that in order to promote stability in managing universities it is imperative that the demands of the various interest groups in the university be seriously and honestly addressed, that decision making in all the structures of the university be democratised and that dialogue between the University Administration and the various interest groups be encouraged and that adequate financial resources be made available to support the needs of the human resources.

Bibliography

Association of African Universities, (1991), *Study on Cost Effectiveness and Efficiency in African Universities*, Accra, Ghana: Association of African Universities.

Baregu, M. (1991), *University Management Administration and the Imperative of the Academy:* UDASA newsletter, 13 July.

Commonwealth Secretariat, (1992), *Eduardo Mondlane University: Review of Governance, Planning and Management*, London Commonwealth Secretariat, Special Commonwealth Fund for Mozambique.

Coombe, Trevor, (1991), *A Consultation on Higher Education in Africa II A Report to the Ford Foundation and the Rockfeller Foundation.* New York, The Ford Foundation.

Goma, Lameck K H., (1989), "The Crisis in Higher Education in Africa" Discovery and Innovation.

Mwiria, Kilemi, (1992), *University Governance: Problems and Prospects in Anglophone Africa* World Bank, Washington DC.

N'dri, Theresa Assie-Lumumba, (1993), *Higher Education in Francophone Africa: Assessment of the Potential of the Traditional Universities and alternatives for development.* World Bank, Washington D.C.

Omiri, I.M. and Mihyo, P. B, (1991), *The Roots of Student Unrest in Africa Universities* Man Graphics Ltd, Nairobi, Kenya.

Saint William S, (1992), *Universities in Africa Strategies for stabilisation and Revitalisation.* World Bank, Washington D.C.

Zambia, Republic of, (1992), *University Act 1992*, Lusaka.

Epilogue

Herrick C Mpuku and Ivan Zyuulu

It is generally accepted that development policies in most developing countries have hitherto been experimental in nature. There is not one development strategy that can be universally recommended and applied in developing countries to achieve the desired social and economic goals. there are common features in all these countries, but there are also distinguishing characteristics and peculiarities based on different experiences, cultures, etc over time and space. Each country must understand its own political, economic, social and cultural history as well as the aspirations of its people in developing a socio-economic strategy for the country.

Zambia's socio-economic policy is no exception to the above assertion. In an attempt to develop the country, the Zambian government has tried to implement several policies since independence in 1964 in various social and economic sectors; free education and free health, public provision of shelter and state-controlled land tenure systems, state control of economic activity and *dirigiste* economic policies, among other things. While some recognise the positive features of some past policies, there are detractors who see wastage of resources and misdirection of government effort which could have been better deployed to the benefit of the Zambian society.

The debates about the best policy direction in the various sectors of economic life of the country have continued to rage and have become more intense. These discussions have come to the fore more emphatically with the birth of the Third Republic in 1991, which brought in its wake a new political dispensation of openness and soul-searching in Zambia after two and half decades of political and economic centralisation and humanist-socialist ideology and rhetoric.

The articles presented by the various authors above have been an attempt to contribute to these debates by way of analysing topical issues in the areas of Structural Adjustment, Financial Innovation and Reform, Land Tenure, Land Policy, Housing Policy, Sustainable Development, Health Management and Management of Higher Education. They are not conclusive recommendations of a panacea to Zambia's socio-economic problems; however, by highlighting some of the key issues, and subjecting them to rigorous analysis a more informed approach to policy-making and future academic analysis will be made.

The papers are, therefore, meant to be a point of reference for policy makers, government advisors, donor agencies and academics alike about the possible alternatives to development policy-making as well as comments on some of the policies being undertaken with liberalisation being the main thrust in all socio-economic spheres.

We cannot pass easy judgements about recent history, but factual analyses will generate the kind of information necessary for the policies which will enable us to look to the future and enter the third millennium with confidence and hope for successive generations.

Posterity will judge whether the efforts of the past and the initiatives of the present have been worthwhile and meaningful.

For Product Safety Concerns and Information please contact our EU representative GPSR@taylorandfrancis.com Taylor & Francis Verlag GmbH, Kaufingerstraße 24, 80331 München, Germany

Printed and bound by CPI Group (UK) Ltd, Croydon, CR0 4YY
08/05/2025
01864397-0002